John Bull's Other Island

by

Bernard Shaw

The Echo Library 2006

Published by

The Echo Library

Echo Library
131 High St.
Teddington
Middlesex TW11 8HH

www.echo-library.com

Please report serious faults in the text to complaints@echo-library.com

ISBN 1-40680-158-5

ACT I

GREAT George Street, Westminster, is the address of Doyle and Broadbent, civil engineers. On the threshold one reads that the firm consists of Mr Lawrence Doyle and Mr Thomas Broadbent, and that their rooms are on the first floor. Most of their rooms are private; for the partners, being bachelors and bosom friends, live there; and the door marked Private, next the clerks' office, is their domestic sitting room as well as their reception room for clients. Let me describe it briefly from the point of view of a sparrow on the window sill. The outer door is in the opposite wall, close to the right hand corner. Between this door and the left hand corner is a hatstand and a table consisting of large drawing boards on trestles, with plans, rolls of tracing paper, mathematical instruments and other draughtsman's accessories on it. In the left hand wall is the fireplace, and the door of an inner room between the fireplace and our observant sparrow. Against the right hand wall is a filing cabinet, with a cupboard on it, and, nearer, a tall office desk and stool for one person. In the middle of the room a large double writing table is set across, with a chair at each end for the two partners. It is a room which no woman would tolerate, smelling of tobacco, and much in need of repapering, repainting, and recarpeting; but this is the effect of bachelor untidiness and indifference, not want of means; for nothing that Doyle and Broadbent themselves have purchased is cheap; nor is anything they want lacking. On the walls hang a large map of South America, a pictorial advertisement of a steamship company, an impressive portrait of Gladstone, and several caricatures of Mr Balfour as a rabbit and Mr Chamberlain as a fox by Francis Carruthers Gould.

At twenty minutes to five o'clock on a summer afternoon in 1904, the room is empty. Presently the outer door is opened, and a valet comes in laden with a large Gladstone bag, and a strap of rugs. He carries them into the inner room. He is a respectable valet, old enough to have lost all alacrity, and acquired an air of putting up patiently with a great deal of trouble and indifferent health. The luggage belongs to Broadbent, who enters after the valet. He pulls off his overcoat and hangs it with his hat on the stand. Then he comes to the writing table and looks through the letters which are waiting for him. He is a robust, full-blooded, energetic man in the prime of life, sometimes eager and credulous, sometimes shrewd and roguish, sometimes portentously solemn, sometimes jolly and impetuous, always buoyant and irresistible, mostly likeable, and enormously absurd in his most earnest moments. He bursts open his letters with his thumb, and glances through them, flinging the envelopes about the floor with reckless untidiness whilst he talks to the valet.

BROADBENT [calling] Hodson.

HODSON [in the bedroom] Yes sir.

BROADBENT. Don't unpack. Just take out the things I've worn; and put in clean things.

HODSON [appearing at the bedroom door] Yes sir. [He turns to go back into the bedroom.

BROADBENT. And look here! [Hodson turns again]. Do you remember where I put my revolver?

HODSON. Revolver, sir? Yes sir. Mr Doyle uses it as a paper-weight, sir, when he's drawing.

BROADBENT. Well, I want it packed. There's a packet of cartridges somewhere, I think. Find it and pack it as well.

HODSON. Yes sir.

BROADBENT. By the way, pack your own traps too. I shall take you with me this time.

HODSON [hesitant]. Is it a dangerous part you're going to, sir? Should I be expected to carry a revolver, sir?

BROADBENT. Perhaps it might be as well. I'm going to Ireland.

HODSON [reassured]. Yes sir.

BROADBENT. You don't feel nervous about it, I suppose?

HODSON. Not at all, sir. I'll risk it, sir.

BROADBENT. Have you ever been in Ireland?

HODSON. No sir. I understand it's a very wet climate, sir. I'd better pack your india-rubber overalls.

BROADBENT. Do. Where's Mr Doyle?

HODSON. I'm expecting him at five, sir. He went out after lunch.

BROADBENT. Anybody been looking for me?

HODSON. A person giving the name of Haffigan has called twice to-day, sir.

BROADBENT. Oh, I'm sorry. Why didn't he wait? I told him to wait if I wasn't in.

HODSON. Well Sir, I didn't know you expected him; so I thought it best to—to—not to encourage him, sir.

BROADBENT. Oh, he's all right. He's an Irishman, and not very particular about his appearance.

HODSON. Yes sir, I noticed that he was rather Irish....

BROADBENT. If he calls again let him come up.

HODSON. I think I saw him waiting about, sir, when you drove up. Shall I fetch him, sir?

BROADBENT. Do, Hodson.

HODSON. Yes sir [He makes for the outer door].

BROADBENT. He'll want tea. Let us have some.

HODSON [stopping]. I shouldn't think he drank tea, sir.

BROADBENT. Well, bring whatever you think he'd like.

HODSON. Yes sir [An electric bell rings]. Here he is, sir. Saw you arrive, sir.

BROADBENT. Right. Show him in. [Hodson goes out. Broadbent gets through the rest of his letters before Hodson returns with the visitor].

HODSON. Mr Affigan.

Haffigan is a stunted, shortnecked, smallheaded, redhaired man of about 30, with reddened nose and furtive eyes. He is dressed in seedy black, almost clerically, and might be a tenth-rate schoolmaster ruined by drink. He hastens to shake Broadbent's hand with a show of reckless geniality and high spirits, helped out by a rollicking stage brogue. This is perhaps a comfort to himself, as he is secretly pursued by the horrors of incipient delirium tremens.

HAFFIGAN. Tim Haffigan, sir, at your service. The top o the mornin to you, Misther Broadbent.

BROADBENT [delighted with his Irish visitor]. Good afternoon, Mr Haffigan.

TIM. An is it the afthernoon it is already? Begorra, what I call the mornin is all the time a man fasts afther breakfast.

BROADBENT. Haven't you lunched?

TIM. Divil a lunch!

BROADBENT. I'm sorry I couldn't get back from Brighton in time to offer you some; but—

TIM. Not a word, sir, not a word. Sure it'll do tomorrow. Besides, I'm Irish, sir: a poor ather, but a powerful dhrinker.

BROADBENT. I was just about to ring for tea when you came. Sit down, Mr Haffigan.

TIM. Tay is a good dhrink if your nerves can stand it. Mine can't.

Haffigan sits down at the writing table, with his back to the filing cabinet. Broadbent sits opposite him. Hodson enters emptyhanded; takes two glasses, a siphon, and a tantalus from the cupboard; places them before Broadbent on the writing table; looks ruthlessly at Haffigan, who cannot meet his eye; and retires.

BROADBENT. Try a whisky and soda.

TIM [sobered]. There you touch the national wakeness, sir. [Piously] Not that I share it meself. I've seen too much of the mischief of it.

BROADBENT [pouring the whisky]. Say when.

TIM. Not too sthrong. [Broadbent stops and looks enquiringly at him]. Say half-an-half. [Broadbent, somewhat startled by this demand, pours a little more, and again stops and looks]. Just a dhrain more: the lower half o the tumbler doesn't hold a fair half. Thankya.

BROADBENT [laughing]. You Irishmen certainly do know how to drink. [Pouring some whisky for himself] Now that's my poor English idea of a whisky and soda.

TIM. An a very good idea it is too. Dhrink is the curse o me unhappy counthry. I take it meself because I've a wake heart and a poor digestion; but in principle I'm a teetoatler.

BROADBENT [suddenly solemn and strenuous]. So am I, of course. I'm a Local Optionist to the backbone. You have no idea, Mr Haffigan, of the ruin that is wrought in this country by the unholy alliance of the publicans, the bishops, the Tories, and The Times. We must close the public-houses at all costs [he drinks].

TIM. Sure I know. It's awful [he drinks]. I see you're a good Liberal like meself, sir.

BROADBENT. I am a lover of liberty, like every true Englishman, Mr

Haffigan. My name is Broadbent. If my name were Breitstein, and I had a hooked nose and a house in Park Lane, I should carry a Union Jack handkerchief and a penny trumpet, and tax the food of the people to support the Navy League, and clamor for the destruction of the last remnants of national liberty—

TIM. Not another word. Shake hands.

BROADBENT. But I should like to explain—

TIM. Sure I know every word you're goin to say before yev said it. I know the sort o man yar. An so you're thinkin o comin to Ireland for a bit?

BROADBENT. Where else can I go? I am an Englishman and a Liberal; and now that South Africa has been enslaved and destroyed, there is no country left to me to take an interest in but Ireland. Mind: I don't say that an Englishman has not other duties. He has a duty to Finland and a duty to Macedonia. But what sane man can deny that an Englishman's first duty is his duty to Ireland? Unfortunately, we have politicians here more unscrupulous than Bobrikoff, more bloodthirsty than Abdul the Damned; and it is under their heel that Ireland is now writhing.

TIM. Faith, they've reckoned up with poor oul Bobrikoff anyhow.

BROADBENT. Not that I defend assassination: God forbid! However strongly we may feel that the unfortunate and patriotic young man who avenged the wrongs of Finland on the Russian tyrant was perfectly right from his own point of view, yet every civilized man must regard murder with abhorrence. Not even in defence of Free Trade would I lift my hand against a political opponent, however richly he might deserve it.

TIM. I'm sure you wouldn't; and I honor you for it. You're goin to Ireland, then, out o sympithy: is it?

BROADBENT. I'm going to develop an estate there for the Land Development Syndicate, in which I am interested. I am convinced that all it needs to make it pay is to handle it properly, as estates are handled in England. You know the English plan, Mr Haffigan, don't you?

TIM. Bedad I do, sir. Take all you can out of Ireland and spend it in England: that's it.

BROADBENT [not quite liking this]. My plan, sir, will be to take a little money out of England and spend it in Ireland.

TIM. More power to your elbow! an may your shadda never be less! for you're the broth of a boy intirely. An how can I help you? Command me to the last dhrop o me blood.

BROADBENT. Have you ever heard of Garden City?

TIM [doubtfully]. D'ye mane Heavn?

BROADBENT. Heaven! No: it's near Hitchin. If you can spare half an hour I'll go into it with you.

TIM. I tell you hwat. Gimme a prospectus. Lemme take it home and reflect on it.

BROADBENT. You're quite right: I will. [He gives him a copy of Mr Ebenezer Howard's book, and several pamphlets]. You understand that the map of the city—the circular construction—is only a suggestion.

TIM. I'll make a careful note o that [looking dazedly at the map].

BROADBENT. What I say is, why not start a Garden City in Ireland?

TIM [with enthusiasm]. That's just what was on the tip o me tongue to ask you. Why not? [Defiantly] Tell me why not.

BROADBENT. There are difficulties. I shall overcome them; but there are difficulties. When I first arrive in Ireland I shall be hated as an Englishman. As a Protestant, I shall be denounced from every altar. My life may be in danger. Well, I am prepared to face that.

TIM. Never fear, sir. We know how to respict a brave innimy.

BROADBENT. What I really dread is misunderstanding. I think you could help me to avoid that. When I heard you speak the other evening in Bermondsey at the meeting of the National League, I saw at once that you were—You won't mind my speaking frankly?

TIM. Tell me all me faults as man to man. I can stand anything but flatthery.

BROADBENT. May I put it in this way?—that I saw at once that you were a thorough Irishman, with all the faults and all, the qualities of your race: rash and improvident but brave and goodnatured; not likely to succeed in business on your own account perhaps, but eloquent, humorous, a lover of freedom, and a true follower of that great Englishman Gladstone.

TIM. Spare me blushes. I mustn't sit here to be praised to me face. But I confess to the goodnature: it's an Irish wakeness. I'd share me last shillin with a friend.

BROADBENT. I feel sure you would, Mr Haffigan.

TIM [impulsively]. Damn it! call me Tim. A man that talks about Ireland as you do may call me anything. Gimme a howlt o that whisky bottle [he replenishes].

BROADBENT [smiling indulgently]. Well, Tim, will you come with me and help to break the ice between me and your warmhearted, impulsive countrymen?

TIM. Will I come to Madagascar or Cochin China wid you? Bedad I'll come to the North Pole wid you if yll pay me fare; for the divil a shillin I have to buy a third class ticket.

BROADBENT. I've not forgotten that, Tim. We must put that little matter on a solid English footing, though the rest can be as Irish as you please. You must come as my—my—well, I hardly know what to call it. If we call you my agent, they'll shoot you. If we call you a bailiff, they'll duck you in the horsepond. I have a secretary already; and—

TIM. Then we'll call him the Home Secretary and me the Irish Secretary. Eh?

BROADBENT [laughing industriously]. Capital. Your Irish wit has settled the first difficulty. Now about your salary—

TIM. A salary, is it? Sure I'd do it for nothin, only me cloes ud disgrace you; and I'd be dhriven to borra money from your friends: a thing that's agin me nacher. But I won't take a penny more than a hundherd a year. [He looks with restless cunning at Broadbent, trying to guess how far he may go].

BROADBENT. If that will satisfy you—

TIM [more than reassured]. Why shouldn't it satisfy me? A hundherd a year is twelve-pound a month, isn't it?

BROADBENT. No. Eight pound six and eightpence.

TIM. Oh murdher! An I'll have to sind five timme poor oul mother in Ireland. But no matther: I said a hundherd; and what I said I'll stick to, if I have to starve for it.

BROADBENT [with business caution]. Well, let us say twelve pounds for the first month. Afterwards, we shall see how we get on.

TIM. You're a gentleman, sir. Whin me mother turns up her toes, you shall take the five pounds off; for your expinses must be kep down wid a sthrong hand; an—[He is interrupted by the arrival of Broadbent's partner.]

Mr Laurence Doyle is a man of 36, with cold grey eyes, strained nose, fine fastidious lips, critical brown, clever head, rather refined and goodlooking on the whole, but with a suggestion of thinskinedness and dissatisfaction that contrasts strongly with Broadbent's eupeptic jollity.

He comes in as a man at home there, but on seeing the stranger shrinks at once, and is about to withdraw when Broadbent reassures him. He then comes forward to the table, between the two others.

DOYLE [retreating]. You're engaged.

BROADBENT. Not at all, not at all. Come in. [To Tim] This gentleman is a friend who lives with me here: my partner, Mr Doyle. [To Doyle] This is a new Irish friend of mine, Mr Tim Haffigan.

TIM [rising with effusion]. Sure it's meself that's proud to meet any friend o Misther Broadbent's. The top o the mornin to you, sir! Me heart goes out teeye both. It's not often I meet two such splendid speciments iv the Anglo-Saxon race.

BROADBENT [chuckling] Wrong for once, Tim. My friend Mr Doyle is a countryman of yours.

Tim is noticeably dashed by this announcement. He draws in his horns at once, and scowls suspiciously at Doyle under a vanishing mark of goodfellowship: cringing a little, too, in mere nerveless fear of him.

DOYLE [with cool disgust]. Good evening. [He retires to the fireplace, and says to Broadbent in a tone which conveys the strongest possible hint to Haffigan that he is unwelcome] Will you soon be disengaged?

TIM [his brogue decaying into a common would-be genteel accent with an unexpected strain of Glasgow in it]. I must be going. Ivnmportnt engeegement in the west end.

BROADBENT [rising]. It's settled, then, that you come with me.

TIM. Ish'll be verra pleased to accompany ye, sir.

BROADBENT. But how soon? Can you start tonight—from Paddington? We go by Milford Haven.

TIM [hesitating]. Well—I'm afreed—I [Doyle goes abruptly into the bedroom, slamming the door and shattering the last remnant of Tim's nerve. The poor wretch saves himself from bursting into tears by plunging again into his role of daredevil Irishman. He rushes to Broadbent; plucks at his sleeve with trembling fingers; and pours forth his entreaty with all the brogue be can muster, subduing his voice lest Doyle should hear and return]. Misther Broadbent: don't humiliate me before a fella counthryman. Look here: me cloes is up the spout. Gimme a fypounnote—I'll pay ya nex choosda whin me ship comes home—or you can stop it out o me month's sallery. I'll be on the platform at Paddnton punctial an ready. Gimme it quick, before he comes back. You won't mind me axin, will ye?

BROADBENT. Not at all. I was about to offer you an advance for travelling expenses. [He gives him a bank note].

TIM [pocketing it]. Thank you. I'll be there half an hour before the thrain starts. [Larry is heard at the bedroom door, returning]. Whisht: he's comin back. Goodbye an God bless ye. [He hurries out almost crying, the 5 pound note and all the drink it means to him being too much for his empty stomach and overstrained nerves].

DOYLE [returning]. Where the devil did you pick up that seedy swindler? What was he doing here? [He goes up to the table where the plans are, and makes a note on one of them, referring to his pocket book as he does so].

BROADBENT. There you go! Why are you so down on every Irishman you meet, especially if he's a bit shabby? poor devil! Surely a fellow-countryman may pass you the top of the morning without offence, even if his coat is a bit shiny at the seams.

DOYLE [contemptuously]. The top of the morning! Did he call you the broth of a boy? [He comes to the writing table].

BROADBENT [triumphantly]. Yes.

DOYLE. And wished you more power to your elbow?

BROADBENT. He did.

DOYLE. And that your shadow might never be less?

BROADBENT. Certainly.

DOYLE [taking up the depleted whisky bottle and shaking his head at it]. And he got about half a pint of whisky out of you.

BROADBENT. It did him no harm. He never turned a hair.

DOYLE. How much money did he borrow?

BROADBENT. It was not borrowing exactly. He showed a very honorable spirit about money. I believe he would share his last shilling with a friend.

DOYLE. No doubt he would share his friend's last shilling if his friend was fool enough to let him. How much did he touch you for?

BROADBENT. Oh, nothing. An advance on his salary—for travelling expenses.

DOYLE. Salary! In Heaven's name, what for?

BROADBENT. For being my Home Secretary, as he very wittily called it.

DOYLE. I don't see the joke.

BROADBENT. You can spoil any joke by being cold blooded about it. I saw it all right when he said it. It was something—something really very amusing—about the Home Secretary and the Irish Secretary. At all events, he's evidently the very man to take with me to Ireland to break the ice for me. He can gain the confidence of the people there, and make them friendly to me. Eh? [He seats himself on the office stool, and tilts it back so that the edge of the standing desk supports his back and prevents his toppling over].

DOYLE. A nice introduction, by George! Do you suppose the whole population of Ireland consists of drunken begging letter writers, or that even if it did, they would accept one another as references?

BROADBENT. Pooh! nonsense! He's only an Irishman. Besides, you don't seriously suppose that Haffigan can humbug me, do you?

DOYLE. No: he's too lazy to take the trouble. All he has to do is to sit there and drink your whisky while you humbug yourself. However, we needn't argue about Haffigan, for two reasons. First, with your money in his pocket he will never reach Paddington: there are too many public houses on the way. Second, he's not an Irishman at all.

BROADBENT. Not an Irishman! [He is so amazed by the statement that he straightens himself and brings the stool bolt upright].

DOYLE. Born in Glasgow. Never was in Ireland in his life. I know all about him.

BROADBENT. But he spoke—he behaved just like an Irishman.

DOYLE. Like an Irishman!! Is it possible that you don't know that all this top-o-the-morning and broth-of-a-boy and more-power-to- your-elbow business is as peculiar to England as the Albert Hall concerts of Irish music are? No Irishman ever talks like that in Ireland, or ever did, or ever will. But when a thoroughly worthless Irishman comes to England, and finds the whole place full of romantic duffers like you, who will let him loaf and drink and sponge and brag as long as he flatters your sense of moral superiority by playing the fool and degrading himself and his country, he soon learns the antics that take you in. He picks them up at the theatre or the music hall. Haffigan learnt the rudiments from his father, who came from my part of Ireland. I knew his uncles, Matt and Andy Haffigan of Rosscullen.

BROADBENT [still incredulous]. But his brogue!

DOYLE. His brogue! A fat lot you know about brogues! I've heard you call a Dublin accent that you could hang your hat on, a brogue. Heaven help you! you don't know the difference between Connemara and Rathmines. [With violent irritation] Oh, damn Tim Haffigan! Let's drop the subject: he's not worth wrangling about.

BROADBENT. What's wrong with you today, Larry? Why are you so bitter?

Doyle looks at him perplexedly; comes slowly to the writing table; and sits down at the end next the fireplace before replying.

DOYLE. Well: your letter completely upset me, for one thing.

BROADBENT. Why?

LARRY. Your foreclosing this Rosscullen mortgage and turning poor Nick Lestrange out of house and home has rather taken me aback; for I liked the old rascal when I was a boy and had the run of his park to play in. I was brought up on the property.

BROADBENT. But he wouldn't pay the interest. I had to foreclose on behalf of the Syndicate. So now I'm off to Rosscullen to look after the property myself. [He sits down at the writing table opposite Larry, and adds, casually, but with an anxious glance at his partner] You're coming with me, of course?

DOYLE [rising nervously and recommencing his restless movements]. That's it. That's what I dread. That's what has upset me.

BROADBENT. But don't you want to see your country again after 18 years absence? to see your people, to be in the old home again? To—

DOYLE [interrupting him very impatiently]. Yes, yes: I know all that as well as you do.

BROADBENT. Oh well, of course [with a shrug] if you take it in that way, I'm sorry.

DOYLE. Never you mind my temper: it's not meant for you, as you ought to know by this time. [He sits down again, a little ashamed of his petulance; reflects a moment bitterly; then bursts out] I have an instinct against going back to Ireland: an instinct so strong that I'd rather go with you to the South Pole than to Rosscullen.

BROADBENT. What! Here you are, belonging to a nation with the strongest patriotism! the most inveterate homing instinct in the world! and you pretend you'd rather go anywhere than back to Ireland. You don't suppose I believe you, do you? In your heart—

DOYLE. Never mind my heart: an Irishman's heart is nothing but his imagination. How many of all those millions that have left Ireland have ever come back or wanted to come back? But what's the use of talking to you? Three verses of twaddle about the Irish emigrant "sitting on the stile, Mary," or three hours of Irish patriotism in Bermondsey or the Scotland Division of Liverpool, go further with you than all the facts that stare you in the face. Why, man alive, look at me! You know the way I nag, and worry, and carp, and cavil, and disparage, and am never satisfied and never quiet, and try the patience of my best friends.

BROADBENT. Oh, come, Larry! do yourself justice. You're very amusing and agreeable to strangers.

DOYLE. Yes, to strangers. Perhaps if I was a bit stiffer to strangers, and a bit easier at home, like an Englishman, I'd be better company for you.

BROADBENT. We get on well enough. Of course you have the melancholy of the Celtic race—

DOYLE [bounding out of his chair] Good God!!!

BROADBENT [slyly]—and also its habit of using strong language when there's nothing the matter.

DOYLE. Nothing the matter! When people talk about the Celtic race, I feel as if I could burn down London. That sort of rot does more harm than ten Coercion Acts. Do you suppose a man need be a Celt to feel melancholy in Rosscullen? Why, man, Ireland was peopled just as England was; and its breed was crossed by just the same invaders.

BROADBENT. True. All the capable people in Ireland are of English extraction. It has often struck me as a most remarkable circumstance that the only party in parliament which shows the genuine old English character and spirit is the Irish party. Look at its independence, its determination, its defiance of bad Governments, its sympathy with oppressed nationalities all the world over! How English!

DOYLE. Not to mention the solemnity with which it talks old- fashioned nonsense which it knows perfectly well to be a century behind the times. That's English, if you like.

BROADBENT. No, Larry, no. You are thinking of the modern hybrids that now monopolize England. Hypocrites, humbugs, Germans, Jews, Yankees, foreigners, Park Laners, cosmopolitan riffraff. Don't call them English. They don't belong to the dear old island, but to their confounded new empire; and by George! they're worthy of it; and I wish them joy of it.

DOYLE [unmoved by this outburst]. There! You feel better now, don't you?

BROADBENT [defiantly]. I do. Much better.

DOYLE. My dear Tom, you only need a touch of the Irish climate to be as big a fool as I am myself. If all my Irish blood were poured into your veins, you wouldn't turn a hair of your constitution and character. Go and marry the most English Englishwoman you can find, and then bring up your son in Rosscullen; and that son's character will be so like mine and so unlike yours that everybody will accuse me of being his father. [With sudden anguish] Rosscullen! oh, good Lord, Rosscullen! The dullness! the hopelessness! the ignorance! the bigotry!

BROADBENT [matter-of-factly]. The usual thing in the country, Larry. Just the same here.

DOYLE [hastily]. No, no: the climate is different. Here, if the life is dull, you can be dull too, and no great harm done. [Going off into a passionate dream] But your wits can't thicken in that soft moist air, on those white springy roads, in those misty rushes and brown bogs, on those hillsides of granite rocks and magenta heather. You've no such colors in the sky, no such lure in the distances, no such sadness in the evenings. Oh, the dreaming! the dreaming! the torturing, heartscalding, never satisfying dreaming, dreaming, dreaming, dreaming! [Savagely] No debauchery that ever coarsened and brutalized an Englishman can take the worth and usefulness out of him like that dreaming. An Irishman's imagination never lets him alone, never convinces him, never satisfies him; but it makes him that he can't face reality nor deal with it nor handle it nor conquer it: he can only sneer at them that do, and [bitterly, at Broadbent] be "agreeable to strangers," like a good-for-nothing woman on the streets. [Gabbling at Broadbent across the table] It's all dreaming, all imagination. He can't be religious. The inspired Churchman that teaches him the sanctity of life and the importance of conduct is sent away empty; while the poor village priest that gives him a miracle or a sentimental story of a saint, has cathedrals built for him out of the pennies of the poor. He can't be intelligently political, he dreams of what the Shan Van Vocht said in ninety- eight. If you want to interest him in

Ireland you've got to call the unfortunate island Kathleen ni Hoolihan and pretend she's a little old woman. It saves thinking. It saves working. It saves everything except imagination, imagination, imagination; and imagination's such a torture that you can't bear it without whisky. [With fierce shivering self-contempt] At last you get that you can bear nothing real at all: you'd rather starve than cook a meal; you'd rather go shabby and dirty than set your mind to take care of your clothes and wash yourself; you nag and squabble at home because your wife isn't an angel, and she despises you because you're not a hero; and you hate the whole lot round you because they're only poor slovenly useless devils like yourself. [Dropping his voice like a man making some shameful confidence] And all the while there goes on a horrible, senseless, mischievous laughter. When you're young, you exchange drinks with other young men; and you exchange vile stories with them; and as you're too futile to be able to help or cheer them, you chaff and sneer and taunt them for not doing the things you daren't do yourself. And all the time you laugh, laugh, laugh! eternal derision, eternal envy, eternal folly, eternal fouling and staining and degrading, until, when you come at last to a country where men take a question seriously and give a serious answer to it, you deride them for having no sense of humor, and plume yourself on your own worthlessness as if it made you better than them.

BROADBENT [roused to intense earnestness by Doyle's eloquence]. Never despair, Larry. There are great possibilities for Ireland. Home Rule will work wonders under English guidance.

DOYLE [pulled up short, his face twitching with a reluctant smile]. Tom: why do you select my most tragic moments for your most irresistible strokes of humor?

BROADBENT. Humor! I was perfectly serious. What do you mean? Do you doubt my seriousness about Home Rule?

DOYLE. I am sure you are serious, Tom, about the English guidance.

BROADBENT [quite reassured]. Of course I am. Our guidance is the important thing. We English must place our capacity for government without stint at the service of nations who are less fortunately endowed in that respect; so as to allow them to develop in perfect freedom to the English level of self-government, you know. You understand me?

DOYLE. Perfectly. And Rosscullen will understand you too.

BROADBENT [cheerfully]. Of course it will. So that's all right. [He pulls up his chair and settles himself comfortably to lecture Doyle]. Now, Larry, I've listened carefully to all you've said about Ireland; and I can see nothing whatever to prevent your coming with me. What does it all come to? Simply that you were only a young fellow when you were in Ireland. You'll find all that chaffing and drinking and not knowing what to be at in Peckham just the same as in Donnybrook. You looked at Ireland with a boy's eyes and saw only boyish things. Come back with me and look at it with a man's, and get a better opinion of your country.

DOYLE. I daresay you're partly right in that: at all events I know very well that if I had been the son of a laborer instead of the son of a country landagent,

I should have struck more grit than I did. Unfortunately I'm not going back to visit the Irish nation, but to visit my father and Aunt Judy and Nora Reilly and Father Dempsey and the rest of them.

BROADBENT. Well, why not? They'll be delighted to see you, now that England has made a man of you.

DOYLE [struck by this]. Ah! you hit the mark there, Tom, with true British inspiration.

BROADBENT. Common sense, you mean.

DOYLE [quickly]. No I don't: you've no more common sense than a gander. No Englishman has any common sense, or ever had, or ever will have. You're going on a sentimental expedition for perfectly ridiculous reasons, with your head full of political nonsense that would not take in any ordinarily intelligent donkey; but you can hit me in the eye with the simple truth about myself and my father.

BROADBENT [amazed]. I never mentioned your father.

DOYLE [not heeding the interruption]. There he is in Rosscullen, a landagent who's always been in a small way because he's a Catholic, and the landlords are mostly Protestants. What with land courts reducing rents and Land Acts turning big estates into little holdings, he'd be a beggar this day if he hadn't bought his own little farm under the Land Purchase Act. I doubt if he's been further from home than Athenmullet for the last twenty years. And here am I, made a man of, as you say, by England.

BROADBENT [apologetically]. I assure you I never meant—

DOYLE. Oh, don't apologize: it's quite true. I daresay I've learnt something in America and a few other remote and inferior spots; but in the main it is by living with you and working in double harness with you that I have learnt to live in a real world and not in an imaginary one. I owe more to you than to any Irishman.

BROADBENT [shaking his head with a twinkle in his eye]. Very friendly of you, Larry, old man, but all blarney. I like blarney; but it's rot, all the same.

DOYLE. No it's not. I should never have done anything without you; although I never stop wondering at that blessed old head of yours with all its ideas in watertight compartments, and all the compartments warranted impervious to anything that it doesn't suit you to understand.

BROADBENT [invincible]. Unmitigated rot, Larry, I assure you.

DOYLE. Well, at any rate you will admit that all my friends are either Englishmen or men of the big world that belongs to the big Powers. All the serious part of my life has been lived in that atmosphere: all the serious part of my work has been done with men of that sort. Just think of me as I am now going back to Rosscullen! to that hell of littleness and monotony! How am I to get on with a little country landagent that ekes out his 5 per cent with a little farming and a scrap of house property in the nearest country town? What am I to say to him? What is he to say to me?

BROADBFNT [scandalized]. But you're father and son, man!

DOYLE. What difference does that make? What would you say if I proposed a visit to YOUR father?

BROADBENT [with filial rectitude]. I always made a point of going to see my father regularly until his mind gave way.

DOYLE [concerned]. Has he gone mad? You never told me.

BROADBENT. He has joined the Tariff Reform League. He would never have done that if his mind had not been weakened. [Beginning to declaim] He has fallen a victim to the arts of a political charlatan who—

DOYLE [interrupting him]. You mean that you keep clear of your father because he differs from you about Free Trade, and you don't want to quarrel with him. Well, think of me and my father! He's a Nationalist and a Separatist. I'm a metallurgical chemist turned civil engineer. Now whatever else metallurgical chemistry may be, it's not national. It's international. And my business and yours as civil engineers is to join countries, not to separate them. The one real political conviction that our business has rubbed into us is that frontiers are hindrances and flags confounded nuisances.

BROADBENT [still smarting under Mr Chamberlain's economic heresy]. Only when there is a protective tariff—

DOYLE [firmly] Now look here, Tom: you want to get in a speech on Free Trade; and you're not going to do it: I won't stand it. My father wants to make St George's Channel a frontier and hoist a green flag on College Green; and I want to bring Galway within 3 hours of Colchester and 24 of New York. I want Ireland to be the brains and imagination of a big Commonwealth, not a Robinson Crusoe island. Then there's the religious difficulty. My Catholicism is the Catholicism of Charlemagne or Dante, qualified by a great deal of modern science and folklore which Father Dempsey would call the ravings of an Atheist. Well, my father's Catholicism is the Catholicism of Father Dempsey.

BROADBENT [shrewdly]. I don't want to interrupt you, Larry; but you know this is all gammon. These differences exist in all families; but the members rub on together all right. [Suddenly relapsing into portentousness] Of course there are some questions which touch the very foundations of morals; and on these I grant you even the closest relationships cannot excuse any compromise or laxity. For instance—

DOYLE [impatiently springing up and walking about]. For instance, Home Rule, South Africa, Free Trade, and the Education Rate. Well, I should differ from my father on every one of them, probably, just as I differ from you about them.

BROADBENT. Yes; but you are an Irishman; and these things are not serious to you as they are to an Englishman.

DOYLE. What! not even Home Rule!

BROADBENT [steadfastly]. Not even Home Rule. We owe Home Rule not to the Irish, but to our English Gladstone. No, Larry: I can't help thinking that there's something behind all this.

DOYLE [hotly]. What is there behind it? Do you think I'm humbugging you?

BROADBENT. Don't fly out at me, old chap. I only thought—

DOYLE. What did you think?

BROADBENT. Well, a moment ago I caught a name which is new to me: a Miss Nora Reilly, I think. [Doyle stops dead and stares at him with something like awe]. I don't wish to be impertinent, as you know, Larry; but are you sure she has nothing to do with your reluctance to come to Ireland with me?

DOYLE [sitting down again, vanquished]. Thomas Broadbent: I surrender. The poor silly-clever Irishman takes off his hat to God's Englishman. The man who could in all seriousness make that recent remark of yours about Home Rule and Gladstone must be simply the champion idiot of all the world. Yet the man who could in the very next sentence sweep away all my special pleading and go straight to the heart of my motives must be a man of genius. But that the idiot and the genius should be the same man! how is that possible? [Springing to his feet] By Jove, I see it all now. I'll write an article about it, and send it to Nature.

BROADBENT [staring at him]. What on earth—

DOYLE. It's quite simple. You know that a
caterpillar—

BROADBENT. A caterpillar!!!

DOYLE. Yes, a caterpillar. Now give your mind to what I am going to say; for it's a new and important scientific theory of the English national character. A caterpillar—

BROADBENT. Look here, Larry: don't be an ass.

DOYLE [insisting]. I say a caterpillar and I mean a caterpillar. You'll understand presently. A caterpillar [Broadbent mutters a slight protest, but does not press it] when it gets into a tree, instinctively makes itself look exactly like a leaf; so that both its enemies and its prey may mistake it for one and think it not worth bothering about.

BROADBENT. What's that got to do with our English national character?

DOYLE. I'll tell you. The world is as full of fools as a tree is full of leaves. Well, the Englishman does what the caterpillar does. He instinctively makes himself look like a fool, and eats up all the real fools at his ease while his enemies let him alone and laugh at him for being a fool like the rest. Oh, nature is cunning, cunning! [He sits down, lost in contemplation of his word-picture].

BROADBENT [with hearty admiration]. Now you know, Larry, that would never have occurred to me. You Irish people are amazingly clever. Of course it's all tommy rot; but it's so brilliant, you know! How the dickens do you think of such things! You really must write an article about it: they'll pay you something for it. If Nature won't have it, I can get it into Engineering for you: I know the editor.

DOYLE. Let's get back to business. I'd better tell you about Nora Reilly.

BROADBENT. No: never mind. I shouldn't have alluded to her.

DOYLE. I'd rather. Nora has a fortune.

BROADBENT [keenly interested]. Eh? How much?

DOYLE. Forty per annum.

BROADBENT. Forty thousand?

DOYLE. No, forty. Forty pounds.

BROADBENT [much dashed.] That's what you call a fortune in Rosscullen, is it?

DOYLE. A girl with a dowry of five pounds calls it a fortune in Rosscullen. What's more 40 pounds a year IS a fortune there; and Nora Reilly enjoys a good deal of social consideration as an heiress on the strength of it. It has helped my father's household through many a tight place. My father was her father's agent. She came on a visit to us when he died, and has lived with us ever since.

BROADBENT [attentively, beginning to suspect Larry of misconduct with Nora, and resolving to get to the bottom of it]. Since when? I mean how old were you when she came?

DOYLE. I was seventeen. So was she: if she'd been older she'd have had more sense than to stay with us. We were together for 18 months before I went up to Dublin to study. When I went home for Christmas and Easter, she was there: I suppose it used to be something of an event for her, though of course I never thought of that then.

BROADBENT. Were you at all hard hit?

DOYLE. Not really. I had only two ideas at that time, first, to learn to do something; and then to get out of Ireland and have a chance of doing it. She didn't count. I was romantic about her, just as I was romantic about Byron's heroines or the old Round Tower of Rosscullen; but she didn't count any more than they did. I've never crossed St George's Channel since for her sake—never even landed at Queenstown and come back to London through Ireland.

BROADBENT. But did you ever say anything that would justify her in waiting for you?

DOYLE. No, never. But she IS waiting for me.

BROADBENT. How do you know?

DOYLE. She writes to me—on her birthday. She used to write on mine, and send me little things as presents; but I stopped that by pretending that it was no use when I was travelling, as they got lost in the foreign post-offices. [He pronounces post-offices with the stress on offices, instead of on post].

BROADBENT. You answer the letters?

DOYLE. Not very punctually. But they get acknowledged at one time or another.

BROADBENT. How do you feel when you see her handwriting?

DOYLE. Uneasy. I'd give 50 pounds to escape a letter.

BROADBENT [looking grave, and throwing himself back in his chair to intimate that the cross-examination is over, and the result very damaging to the witness] Hm!

DOYLE. What d'ye mean by Hm!?

BROADBENT. Of course I know that the moral code is different in Ireland. But in England it's not considered fair to trifle with a woman's affections.

DOYLE. You mean that an Englishman would get engaged to another woman and return Nora her letters and presents with a letter to say he was unworthy of her and wished her every happiness?

BROADBENT. Well, even that would set the poor girl's mind at rest.

DOYLE. Would it? I wonder! One thing I can tell you; and that is that Nora would wait until she died of old age sooner than ask my intentions or condescend to hint at the possibility of my having any. You don't know what Irish pride is. England may have knocked a good deal of it out of me; but she's never been in England; and if I had to choose between wounding that delicacy in her and hitting her in the face, I'd hit her in the face without a moment's hesitation.

BROADBENT [who has been nursing his knee and reflecting, apparently rather agreeably]. You know, all this sounds rather interesting. There's the Irish charm about it. That's the worst of you: the Irish charm doesn't exist for you.

DOYLE. Oh yes it does. But it's the charm of a dream. Live in contact with dreams and you will get something of their charm: live in contact with facts and you will get something of their brutality. I wish I could find a country to live in where the facts were not brutal and the dreams not unreal.

BROADBENT [changing his attitude and responding to Doyle's earnestness with deep conviction: his elbows on the table and his hands clenched]. Don't despair, Larry, old boy: things may look black; but there will be a great change after the next election.

DOYLE [jumping up]. Oh get out, you idiot!

BROADBENT [rising also, not a bit snubbed]. Ha! ha! you may laugh; but we shall see. However, don't let us argue about that. Come now! you ask my advice about Miss Reilly?

DOYLE [reddening]. No I don't. Damn your advice! [Softening] Let's have it, all the same.

BROADBENT. Well, everything you tell me about her impresses me favorably. She seems to have the feelings of a lady; and though we must face the fact that in England her income would hardly maintain her in the lower middle class—

DOYLE [interrupting]. Now look here, Tom. That reminds me. When you go to Ireland, just drop talking about the middle class and bragging of belonging to it. In Ireland you're either a gentleman or you're not. If you want to be particularly offensive to Nora, you can call her a Papist; but if you call her a middle-class woman, Heaven help you!

BROADBENT [irrepressible]. Never fear. You're all descended from the ancient kings: I know that. [Complacently] I'm not so tactless as you think, my boy. [Earnest again] I expect to find Miss Reilly a perfect lady; and I strongly advise you to come and have another look at her before you make up your mind about her. By the way, have you a photograph of her?

DOYLE. Her photographs stopped at twenty-five.

BROADBENT [saddened]. Ah yes, I suppose so. [With feeling, severely] Larry: you've treated that poor girl disgracefully.

DOYLE. By George, if she only knew that two men were talking about her like this—!

BROADBENT. She wouldn't like it, would she? Of course not. We ought to be ashamed of ourselves, Larry. [More and more carried away by his new fancy]. You know, I have a sort of presentiment that Miss Really is a very superior woman.

DOYLE [staring hard at him]. Oh you have, have you?

BROADBENT. Yes I have. There is something very touching about the history of this beautiful girl.

DOYLE. Beau—! Oho! Here's a chance for Nora! and for me! [Calling] Hodson.

HODSON [appearing at the bedroom door]. Did you call, sir?

DOYLE. Pack for me too. I'm going to Ireland with Mr Broadbent.

HODSON. Right, sir. [He retires into the bedroom.]

BROADBENT [clapping Doyle on the shoulder]. Thank you, old chap. Thank you.

ACT II

ROSSCULLEN. Westward a hillside of granite rock and heather slopes upward across the prospect from south to north, a huge stone stands on it in a naturally impossible place, as if it had been tossed up there by a giant. Over the brow, in the desolate valley beyond, is a round tower. A lonely white high road trending away westward past the tower loses itself at the foot of the far mountains. It is evening; and there are great breadths of silken green in the Irish sky. The sun is setting.

A man with the face of a young saint, yet with white hair and perhaps 50 years on his back, is standing near the stone in a trance of intense melancholy, looking over the hills as if by mere intensity of gaze he could pierce the glories of the sunset and see into the streets of heaven. He is dressed in black, and is rather more clerical in appearance than most English curates are nowadays; but he does not wear the collar and waistcoat of a parish priest. He is roused from his trance by the chirp of an insect from a tuft of grass in a crevice of the stone. His face relaxes: he turns quietly, and gravely takes off his hat to the tuft, addressing the insect in a brogue which is the jocular assumption of a gentleman and not the natural speech of a peasant.

THE MAN. An is that yourself, Misther Grasshopper? I hope I see you well this fine evenin.

THE GRASSHOPPER [prompt and shrill in answer]. X.X.

THE MAN [encouragingly]. That's right. I suppose now you've come out to make yourself miserable by admyerin the sunset?

THE GRASSHOPPER [sadly]. X.X.

THE MAN. Aye, you're a thrue Irish grasshopper.

THE GRASSHOPPER [loudly]. X.X.X.

THE MAN. Three cheers for ould Ireland, is it? That helps you to face out the misery and the poverty and the torment, doesn't it?

THE GRASSHOPPER [plaintively]. X.X.

THE MAN. Ah, it's no use, me poor little friend. If you could jump as far as a kangaroo you couldn't jump away from your own heart an its punishment. You can only look at Heaven from here: you can't reach it. There! [pointing with his stick to the sunset] that's the gate o glory, isn't it?

THE GRASSHOPPER [assenting]. X.X.

THE MAN. Sure it's the wise grasshopper yar to know that! But tell me this, Misther Unworldly Wiseman: why does the sight of Heaven wring your heart an mine as the sight of holy wather wrings the heart o the divil? What wickedness have you done to bring that curse on you? Here! where are you jumpin to? Where's your manners to go skyrocketin like that out o the box in the middle o your confession [he threatens it with his stick]?

THE GRASSHOPPER [penitently]. X.

THE MAN [lowering the stick]. I accept your apology; but don't do it again. And now tell me one thing before I let you go home to bed. Which would you say this counthry was: hell or purgatory?

THE GRASSHOPPER. X.

THE MAN. Hell! Faith I'm afraid you're right. I wondher what you and me did when we were alive to get sent here.

THE GRASSHOPPER [shrilly]. X.X.

THE MAN [nodding]. Well, as you say, it's a delicate subject; and I won't press it on you. Now off widja.

THE GRASSHOPPER. X.X. [It springs away].

THE MAN [waving his stick] God speed you! [He walks away past the stone towards the brow of the hill. Immediately a young laborer, his face distorted with terror, slips round from behind the stone.

THE LABORER [crossing himself repeatedly]. Oh glory be to God! glory be to God! Oh Holy Mother an all the saints! Oh murdher! murdher! [Beside himself, calling Fadher Keegan! Fadher Keegan]!

THE MAN [turning]. Who's there? What's that? [He comes back and finds the laborer, who clasps his knees] Patsy Farrell! What are you doing here?

PATSY. O for the love o God don't lave me here wi dhe grasshopper. I hard it spakin to you. Don't let it do me any harm, Father darlint.

KEEGAN. Get up, you foolish man, get up. Are you afraid of a poor insect because I pretended it was talking to me?

PATSY. Oh, it was no pretending, Fadher dear. Didn't it give three cheers n say it was a divil out o hell? Oh say you'll see me safe home, Fadher; n put a blessin on me or somethin [he moans with terror].

KEEGAN. What were you doin there, Patsy, listnin? Were you spyin on me?

PATSY. No, Fadher: on me oath an soul I wasn't: I was waitn to meet Masther Larry n carry his luggage from the car; n I fell asleep on the grass; n you woke me talkin to the grasshopper; n I hard its wicked little voice. Oh, d'ye think I'll die before the year's out, Fadher?

KEEGAN. For shame, Patsy! Is that your religion, to be afraid of a little deeshy grasshopper? Suppose it was a divil, what call have you to fear it? If I could ketch it, I'd make you take it home widja in your hat for a penance.

PATSY. Sure, if you won't let it harm me, I'm not afraid, your riverence. [He gets up, a little reassured. He is a callow, flaxen polled, smoothfaced, downy chinned lad, fully grown but not yet fully filled out, with blue eyes and an instinctively acquired air of helplessness and silliness, indicating, not his real character, but a cunning developed by his constant dread of a hostile dominance, which he habitually tries to disarm and tempt into unmasking by pretending to be a much greater fool than he really is. Englishmen think him half-witted, which is exactly what he intends them to think. He is clad in corduroy trousers, unbuttoned waistcoat, and coarse blue striped shirt].

KEEGAN [admonitorily]. Patsy: what did I tell you about callin me Father Keegan an your reverence? What did Father Dempsey tell you about it?

PATSY. Yis, Fadher.

KEEGAN. Father!

PATSY [desperately]. Arra, hwat am I to call you? Fadher Dempsey sez you're not a priest; n we all know you're not a man; n how do we know what ud happen to us if we showed any disrespect to you? N sure they say wanse a priest always a priest.

KEEGAN [sternly]. It's not for the like of you, Patsy, to go behind the instruction of your parish priest and set yourself up to judge whether your Church is right or wrong.

PATSY. Sure I know that, sir.

KEEGAN. The Church let me be its priest as long as it thought me fit for its work. When it took away my papers it meant you to know that I was only a poor madman, unfit and unworthy to take charge of the souls of the people.

PATSY. But wasn't it only because you knew more Latn than Father Dempsey that he was jealous of you?

KEEGAN [scolding him to keep himself from smiling]. How dar you, Patsy Farrell, put your own wicked little spites and foolishnesses into the heart of your priest? For two pins I'd tell him what you just said.

PATSY [coaxing] Sure you wouldn't—

KEEGAN. Wouldn't I? God forgive you! You're little better than a heathen.

PATSY. Deedn I am, Fadher: it's me bruddher the tinsmith in Dublin you're thinkin of. Sure he had to be a freethinker when he larnt a thrade and went to live in the town.

KEEGAN. Well, he'll get to Heaven before you if you're not careful, Patsy. And now you listen to me, once and for all. You'll talk to me and pray for me by the name of Pether Keegan, so you will. And when you're angry and tempted to lift your hand agen the donkey or stamp your foot on the little grasshopper, remember that the donkey's Pether Keegan's brother, and the grasshopper Pether Keegan's friend. And when you're tempted to throw a stone at a sinner or a curse at a beggar, remember that Pether Keegan is a worse sinner and a worse beggar, and keep the stone and the curse for him the next time you meet him. Now say God bless you, Pether, to me before I go, just to practise you a bit.

PATSY. Sure it wouldn't be right, Fadher. I can't—

KEEGAN. Yes you can. Now out with it; or I'll put this stick into your hand an make you hit me with it.

PATSY [throwing himself on his knees in an ecstasy of adoration]. Sure it's your blessin I want, Fadher Keegan. I'll have no luck widhout it.

KEEGAN [shocked]. Get up out o that, man. Don't kneel to me: I'm not a saint.

PATSY [with intense conviction]. Oh in throth yar, sir. [The grasshopper chirps. Patsy, terrified, clutches at Keegan's hands] Don't set it on me, Fadher: I'll do anythin you bid me.

KEEGAN [pulling him up]. You bosthoon, you! Don't you see that it only whistled to tell me Miss Reilly's comin? There! Look at her and pull yourself together for shame. Off widja to the road: you'll be late for the car if you don't make haste [bustling him down the hill]. I can see the dust of it in the gap already.

PATSY. The Lord save us! [He goes down the hill towards the road like a haunted man].

Nora Reilly comes down the hill. A slight weak woman in a pretty muslin print gown [her best], she is a figure commonplace enough to Irish eyes; but on the inhabitants of fatter-fed, crowded, hustling and bustling modern countries she makes a very different impression. The absence of any symptoms of coarseness or hardness or appetite in her, her comparative delicacy of manner and sensibility of apprehension, her thin hands and slender figure, her travel accent, with the caressing plaintive Irish melody of her speech, give her a charm which is all the more effective because, being untravelled, she is unconscious of it, and never dreams of deliberately dramatizing and exploiting it, as the Irishwoman in England does. For Tom Broadbent therefore, an attractive woman, whom he would even call ethereal. To Larry Doyle, an everyday woman fit only for the eighteenth century, helpless, useless, almost sexless, an invalid without the excuse of disease, an incarnation of everything in Ireland that drove him out of it. These judgments have little value and no finality; but they are the judgments on which her fate hangs just at present. Keegan touches his hat to her: he does not take it off.

NORA. Mr Keegan: I want to speak to you a minute if you don't mind.

KEEGAN [dropping the broad Irish vernacular of his speech to Patsy]. An hour if you like, Miss Reilly: you're always welcome. Shall we sit down?

NORA. Thank you. [They sit on the heather. She is shy and anxious; but she comes to the point promptly because she can think of nothing else]. They say you did a gradle o travelling at one time.

KEEGAN. Well you see I'm not a Mnooth man [he means that he was not a student at Maynooth College]. When I was young I admired the older generation of priests that had been educated in Salamanca. So when I felt sure of my vocation I went to Salamanca. Then I walked from Salamanca to Rome, an sted in a monastery there for a year. My pilgrimage to Rome taught me that walking is a better way of travelling than the train; so I walked from Rome to the Sorbonne in Paris; and I wish I could have walked from Paris to Oxford; for I was very sick on the sea. After a year of Oxford I had to walk to Jerusalem to walk the Oxford feeling off me. From Jerusalem I came back to Patmos, and spent six months at the monastery of Mount Athos. From that I came to Ireland and settled down as a parish priest until I went mad.

NORA [startled]. Oh dons say that.

KEEGAN. Why not? Don't you know the story? how I confessed a black man and gave him absolution; and how he put a spell on me and drove me mad.

NORA. How can you talk such nonsense about yourself? For shame!

KEEGAN. It's not nonsense at all: it's true—in a way. But never mind the black man. Now that you know what a travelled man I am, what can I do for you? [She hesitates and plucks nervously at the heather. He stays her hand gently]. Dear Miss Nora: don't pluck the little flower. If it was a pretty baby you wouldn't want to pull its head off and stick it in a vawse o water to look at. [The grasshopper chirps: Keegan turns his head and addresses it in the vernacular]. Be aisy, me son: she won't spoil the swing-swong in your little three. [To Nora, resuming his urbane style] You see I'm quite cracked; but never mind: I'm harmless. Now what is it?

NORA [embarrassed]. Oh, only idle curiosity. I wanted to know whether you found Ireland—I mean the country part of Ireland, of course—very small and backwardlike when you came back to it from Rome and Oxford and all the great cities.

KEEGAN. When I went to those great cities I saw wonders I had never seen in Ireland. But when I came back to Ireland I found all the wonders there waiting for me. You see they had been there all the time; but my eyes had never been opened to them. I did not know what my own house was like, because I had never been outside it.

NORA. D'ye think that's the same with everybody?

KEEGAN. With everybody who has eyes in his soul as well as in his head.

NORA. But really and truly now, weren't the people rather disappointing? I should think the girls must have seemed rather coarse and dowdy after the foreign princesses and people? But I suppose a priest wouldn't notice that.

KEEGAN. It's a priest's business to notice everything. I won't tell you all I noticed about women; but I'll tell you this. The more a man knows, and the farther he travels, the more likely he is to marry a country girl afterwards.

NORA [blushing with delight]. You're joking, Mr Keegan: I'm sure yar.

KEEGAN. My way of joking is to tell the truth. It's the funniest joke in the world.

NORA [incredulous]. Galong with you!

KEEGAN [springing up actively]. Shall we go down to the road and meet the car? [She gives him her hand and he helps her up]. Patsy Farrell told me you were expecting young Doyle.

NORA [tossing her chin up at once]. Oh, I'm not expecting him particularly. It's a wonder he's come back at all. After staying away eighteen years he can harly expect us to be very anxious to see him, can he now?

KEEGAN. Well, not anxious perhaps; but you will be curious to see how much he has changed in all these years.

NORA [with a sudden bitter flush]. I suppose that's all that brings him back to look at us, just to see how much WE'VE changed. Well, he can wait and see me be candlelight: I didn't come out to meet him: I'm going to walk to the Round Tower [going west across the hill].

KEEGAN. You couldn't do better this fine evening. [Gravely] I'll tell him where you've gone. [She turns as if to forbid him; but the deep understanding in his eyes makes that impossible; and she only looks at him earnestly and goes. He watches her disappear on the other side of the hill; then says] Aye, he's come to torment you; and you're driven already to torment him. [He shakes his head, and goes slowly away across the hill in the opposite direction, lost in thought].

By this time the car has arrived, and dropped three of its passengers on the high road at the foot of the hill. It is a monster jaunting car, black and dilapidated, one of the last survivors of the public vehicles known to earlier generations as Beeyankiny cars, the Irish having laid violent tongues on the name of their projector, one Bianconi, an enterprising Italian. The three passengers are the parish priest, Father Dempsey; Cornelius Doyle, Larry's father; and Broadbent, all in overcoats and as stiff as only an Irish car could make them.

The priest, stout and fatherly, falls far short of that finest type of countryside pastor which represents the genius of priesthood; but he is equally far above the base type in which a strongminded and unscrupulous peasant uses the Church to extort money, power, and privilege. He is a priest neither by vocation nor ambition, but because the life suits him. He has boundless authority over his flock, and taxes them stiffly enough to be a rich man. The old Protestant ascendency is now too broken to gall him. On the whole, an easygoing, amiable, even modest man as long as his dues are paid and his authority and dignity fully admitted.

Cornelius Doyle is an elder of the small wiry type, with a hardskinned, rather worried face, clean shaven except for sandy whiskers blanching into a lustreless pale yellow and quite white at the roots. His dress is that of a country-town titan of business: that is, an oldish shooting suit, and elastic sided boots quite unconnected with shooting. Feeling shy with Broadbent, he is hasty, which is his way of trying to appear genial.

Broadbent, for reasons which will appear later, has no luggage except a field glass and a guide book. The other two have left theirs to the unfortunate Patsy Farrell, who struggles up the hill after them, loaded with a sack of potatoes, a hamper, a fat goose, a colossal salmon, and several paper parcels.

Cornelius leads the way up the hill, with Broadbent at his heels. The priest follows; and Patsy lags laboriously behind.

CORNELIUS. This is a bit of a climb, Mr. Broadbent; but it's shorter than goin round be the road.

BROADBENT [stopping to examine the great stone]. Just a moment, Mr Doyle: I want to look at this stone. It must be Finian's die-cast.

CORNELIUS [in blank bewilderment]. Hwat?

BROADBENT. Murray describes it. One of your great national heroes—I can't pronounce the name—Finian Somebody, I think.

FATHER DEMPSEY [also perplexed, and rather scandalized]. Is it Fin McCool you mean?

BROADBENT. I daresay it is. [Referring to the guide book]. Murray says that a huge stone, probably of Druidic origin, is still pointed out as the die cast by Fin in his celebrated match with the devil.

CORNELIUS [dubiously]. Jeuce a word I ever heard of it!

FATHER DEMPSEY [very seriously indeed, and even a little severely]. Don't believe any such nonsense, sir. There never was any such thing. When people talk to you about Fin McCool and the like, take no notice of them. It's all idle stories and superstition.

BROADBENT [somewhat indignantly; for to be rebuked by an Irish priest for superstition is more than he can stand]. You don't suppose I believe it, do you?

FATHER DEMPSEY. Oh, I thought you did. D'ye see the top o the Roun Tower there? That's an antiquity worth lookin at.

BROADBENT [deeply interested]. Have you any theory as to what the Round Towers were for?

FATHER DEMPSEY [a little offended]. A theory? Me! [Theories are connected in his mind with the late Professor Tyndall, and with scientific scepticism generally: also perhaps with the view that the Round Towers are phallic symbols].

CORNELIUS [remonstrating]. Father Dempsey is the priest of the parish, Mr Broadbent. What would he be doing with a theory?

FATHER DEMPSEY [with gentle emphasis]. I have a KNOWLEDGE of what the Roun Towers were, if that's what you mean. They are the forefingers of the early Church, pointing us all to God.

Patsy, intolerably overburdened, loses his balance, and sits down involuntarily. His burdens are scattered over the hillside. Cornelius and Father Dempsey turn furiously on him, leaving Broadbent beaming at the stone and the tower with fatuous interest.

CORNELIUS. Oh, be the hokey, the sammin's broke in two! You schoopid ass, what d'ye mean?

FATHER DEMPSEY. Are you drunk, Patsy Farrell? Did I tell you to carry that hamper carefully or did I not?

PATSY [rubbing the back of his head, which has almost dented a slab of granite] Sure me fut slpt. Howkn I carry three men's luggage at wanst?

FATHER DEMPSEY. You were told to leave behind what you couldn't carry, an go back for it.

PATSY. An whose things was I to lave behind? Hwat would your reverence think if I left your hamper behind in the wet grass; n hwat would the masther say if I left the sammin and the goose be the side o the road for annywan to pick up?

CORNELIUS. Oh, you've a dale to say for yourself, you, butther-fingered omadhaun. Wait'll Ant Judy sees the state o that sammin: SHE'LL talk to you. Here! gimme that birdn that fish there; an take Father Dempsey's hamper to his house for him; n then come back for the rest.

FATHER DEMPSEY. Do, Patsy. And mind you don't fall down again.

PATSY. Sure I—

CORNELIUS [bustling him up the bill] Whisht! heres Ant Judy. [Patsy goes grumbling in disgrace, with Father Dempsey's hamper].

Aunt Judy comes down the hill, a woman of 50, in no way remarkable, lively and busy without energy or grip, placid without tranquillity, kindly without concern for others: indeed without much concern for herself: a contented product of a narrow, strainless life. She wears her hair parted in the middle and quite smooth, with a fattened bun at the back. Her dress is a plain brown frock, with a woollen pelerine of black and aniline mauve over her shoulders, all very trim in honor of the occasion. She looks round for Larry; is puzzled; then stares incredulously at Broadbent.

AUNT JUDY. Surely to goodness that's not you, Larry!

CORNELIUS. Arra how could he be Larry, woman alive? Larry's in no hurry home, it seems. I haven't set eyes on him. This is his friend, Mr Broadbent. Mr Broadbent, me sister Judy.

AUNT JUDY [hospitably: going to Broadbent and shaking hands heartily]. Mr. Broadbent! Fancy me takin you for Larry! Sure we haven't seen a sight of him for eighteen years, n he only a lad when he left us.

BROADBENT. It's not Larry's fault: he was to have been here before me. He started in our motor an hour before Mr Doyle arrived, to meet us at Athenmullet, intending to get here long before me.

AUNT JUDY. Lord save us! do you think he's had n axidnt?

BROADBENT. No: he's wired to say he's had a breakdown and will come on as soon as he can. He expects to be here at about ten.

AUNT JUDY. There now! Fancy him trustn himself in a motor and we all expectn him! Just like him! he'd never do anything like anybody else. Well, what can't be cured must be injoored. Come on in, all of you. You must be dyin for your tea, Mr Broadbent.

BROADBENT [with a slight start]. Oh, I'm afraid it's too late for tea [he looks at his watch].

AUNT JUDY. Not a bit: we never have it airlier than this. I hope they gave you a good dinner at Athenmullet.

BROADBENT [trying to conceal his consternation as he realizes that he is not going to get any dinner after his drive] Oh—er— excellent, excellent. By the way, hadn't I better see about a room at the hotel? [They stare at him].

CORNELIUS. The hotel!

FATHER DEMPSEY. Hwat hotel?

AUNT JUDY. Indeedn you'e not goin to a hotel. You'll stay with us. I'd have put you into Larry's room, only the boy's pallyass is too short for you; but we'll make a comfortable bed for you on the sofa in the parlor.

BROADBENT. You're very kind, Miss Doyle; but really I'm ashamed to give you so much trouble unnecessarily. I shan't mind the hotel in the least.

FATHER DEMPSEY. Man alive! There's no hotel in Rosscullen.

BROADBENT. No hotel! Why, the driver told me there was the finest hotel in Ireland here. [They regard him joylessly].

AUNT JUDY. Arra would you mind what the like of him would tell you? Sure he'd say hwatever was the least trouble to himself and the pleasantest to you, thinkin you might give him a thruppeny bit for himself or the like.

BROADBENT. Perhaps there's a public house.

FATHER DEMPSEY [grimly.] There's seventeen.

AUNT JUDY. Ah then, how could you stay at a public house? They'd have no place to put you even if it was a right place for you to go. Come! is it the sofa you're afraid of? If it is, you can have me own bed. I can sleep with Nora.

BROADBENT. Not at all, not at all: I should be only too delighted. But to upset your arrangements in this way—

CORNELIUS [anxious to cut short the discussion, which makes him ashamed of his house; for he guesses Broadbent's standard of comfort a little more accurately than his sister does] That's all right: it'll be no trouble at all. Hweres Nora?

AUNT JUDY. Oh, how do I know? She slipped out a little while ago: I thought she was goin to meet the car.

CORNELIUS [dissatisfied] It's a queer thing of her to run out o the way at such a time.

AUNT JUDY. Sure she's a queer girl altogether. Come. Come in, come in.

FATHER DEMPSEY. I'll say good-night, Mr Broadbent. If there's anything I can do for you in this parish, let me know. [He shakes hands with Broadbent].

BROADBENT [effusively cordial]. Thank you, Father Dempsey. Delighted to have met you, sir.

FATHER DEMPSEY [passing on to Aunt Judy]. Good-night, Miss Doyle.

AUNT JUDY. Won't you stay to tea?

FATHER DEMPSEY. Not to-night, thank you kindly: I have business to do at home. [He turns to go, and meets Patsy Farrell returning unloaded]. Have you left that hamper for me?

PATSY. Yis, your reverence.

FATHER DEMPSEY. That's a good lad [going].

PATSY [to Aunt Judy] Fadher Keegan sez—

FATHER DEMPSEY [turning sharply on him]. What's that you say?

PATSY [frightened]. Fadher Keegan—

FATHER DEMPSEY. How often have you heard me bid you call Mister Keegan in his proper name, the same as I do? Father Keegan indeed! Can't you tell the difference between your priest and any ole madman in a black coat?

PATSY. Sure I'm afraid he might put a spell on me.

FATHER DEMPSEY [wrathfully]. You mind what I tell you or I'll put a spell on you that'll make you lep. D'ye mind that now? [He goes home].

Patsy goes down the hill to retrieve the fish, the bird, and the sack.

AUNT JUDY. Ah, hwy can't you hold your tongue, Patsy, before Father Dempsey?

PATSY. Well, what was I to do? Father Keegan bid me tell you Miss Nora was gone to the Roun Tower.

AUNT JUDY. An hwy couldn't you wait to tell us until Father Dempsey was gone?

PATSY. I was afeerd o forgetn it; and then maybe he'd a sent the grasshopper or the little dark looker into me at night to remind me of it. [The dark looker is the common grey lizard, which is supposed to walk down the throats of incautious sleepers and cause them to perish in a slow decline].

CORNELIUS. Yah, you great gaum, you! Widjer grasshoppers and dark lookers! Here: take up them things and let me hear no more o your foolish lip. [Patsy obeys]. You can take the sammin under your oxther. [He wedges the salmon into Patsy's axilla].

PATSY. I can take the goose too, sir. Put it on me back and gimme the neck of it in me mouth. [Cornelius is about to comply thoughtlessly].

AUNT JUDY [feeling that Broadbent's presence demands special punctiliousness]. For shame, Patsy! to offer to take the goose in your mouth that we have to eat after you! The master'll bring it in for you. [Patsy, abashed, yet irritated by this ridiculous fastidiousness, takes his load up the hill].

CORNELIUS. What the jeuce does Nora want to go to the Roun Tower for?

AUNT JUDY. Oh, the Lord knows! Romancin, I suppose. Props she thinks Larry would go there to look for her and see her safe home.

BROADBENT. I'm afraid it's all the fault of my motor. Miss Reilly must not be left to wait and walk home alone at night. Shall I go for her?

AUNT JUDY [contemptuously]. Arra hwat ud happen to her? Hurry in now, Corny. Come, Mr Broadbent. I left the tea on the hob to draw; and it'll be black if we don't go in an drink it.

They go up the hill. It is dark by this time.

Broadbent does not fare so badly after all at Aunt Judy's board. He gets not only tea and bread-and-butter, but more mutton chops than he has ever conceived it possible to eat at one sitting. There is also a most filling substance called potato cake. Hardly have his fears of being starved been replaced by his first misgiving that he is eating too much and will be sorry for it tomorrow, when his appetite is revived by the production of a bottle of illicitly distilled whisky, called pocheen, which he has read and dreamed of [he calls it pottine] and is now at last to taste. His good humor rises almost to excitement before Cornelius shows signs of sleepiness. The contrast between Aunt Judy's table service and that of the south and east coast hotels at which he spends his Fridays-to-Tuesdays when he is in London, seems to him delightfully Irish. The almost total atrophy of any sense of enjoyment in Cornelius, or even any desire for it or toleration of the possibility of life being something better than a round of sordid worries, relieved by tobacco, punch, fine mornings, and petty successes in buying and selling, passes with his guest as the whimsical affectation of a shrewd Irish humorist and incorrigible spendthrift. Aunt Judy seems to him an incarnate joke. The likelihood that the joke will pall after a month or so, and is probably not apparent at any time to born Rossculleners, or that he himself unconsciously entertains Aunt Judy by his fantastic English personality and English mispronunciations, does not occur to him for a moment. In the end he is so charmed, and so loth to go to bed and perhaps dream of prosaic England, that he insists on going out to smoke a cigar and look for Nora Reilly at the Round Tower. Not that any special insistence is needed; for the English inhibitive instinct does not seem to exist in Rosscullen. Just as Nora's liking to miss a meal and stay out at the Round Tower is accepted as a sufficient reason for her doing it, and for the family going to bed and leaving the door open for her, so Broadbent's whim to go out for a late stroll provokes neither hospitable remonstrance nor surprise. Indeed Aunt Judy wants to get rid of him whilst she makes a bed for him on the sofa. So off he goes, full fed, happy and enthusiastic, to explore the valley by moonlight.

The Round Tower stands about half an Irish mile from Rosscullen, some fifty yards south of the road on a knoll with a circle of wild greensward on it. The road once ran over this knoll; but modern engineering has tempered the level to the Beeyankiny car by carrying the road partly round the knoll and partly through a cutting; so that the way from the road to the tower is a footpath up the embankment through furze and brambles.

On the edge of this slope, at the top of the path, Nora is straining her eyes in the moonlight, watching for Larry. At last she gives it up with a sob of impatience, and retreats to the hoary foot of the tower, where she sits down discouraged and cries a little. Then she settles herself resignedly to wait, and hums a song—not an Irish melody, but a hackneyed English drawing-room ballad of the season before last—until some slight noise suggests a footstep, when she springs up eagerly and runs to the edge of the slope again. Some moments of silence and suspense follow, broken by unmistakable footsteps. She gives a little gasp as she sees a man approaching.

NORA. Is that you, Larry? [Frightened a little] Who's that?

[BROADBENT's voice from below on the path]. Don't be alarmed.

NORA. Oh, what an English accent you've got!

BROADBENT [rising into view] I must introduce myself—

NORA [violently startled, retreating]. It's not you! Who are you? What do you want?

BROADBENT [advancing]. I'm really so sorry to have alarmed you, Miss Reilly. My name is Broadbent. Larry's friend, you know.

NORA [chilled]. And has Mr Doyle not come with you?

BROADBENT. No. I've come instead. I hope I am not unwelcome.

NORA [deeply mortified]. I'm sorry Mr Doyle should have given you the trouble, I'm sure.

BROADBENT. You see, as a stranger and an Englishman, I thought it would be interesting to see the Round Tower by moonlight.

NORA. Oh, you came to see the tower. I thought—[confused, trying to recover her manners] Oh, of course. I was so startled—It's a beautiful night, isn't it?

BROADBENT. Lovely. I must explain why Larry has not come himself.

NORA. Why should he come? He's seen the tower often enough: it's no attraction to him. [Genteelly] An what do you think of Ireland, Mr Broadbent? Have you ever been here before?

BROADBENT. Never.

NORA. An how do you like it?

BROADBENT [suddenly betraying a condition of extreme sentimentality]. I can hardly trust myself to say how much I like it. The magic of this Irish scene, and—I really don't want to be personal, Miss Reilly; but the charm of your Irish voice—

NORA [quite accustomed to gallantry, and attaching no seriousness whatever to it]. Oh, get along with you, Mr Broadbent! You're breaking your heart about me already, I daresay, after seeing me for two minutes in the dark.

BROADBENT. The voice is just as beautiful in the dark, you know. Besides, I've heard a great deal about you from Larry.

NORA [with bitter indifference]. Have you now? Well, that's a great honor, I'm sure.

BROADBENT. I have looked forward to meeting you more than to anything else in Ireland.

NORA [ironically]. Dear me! did you now?

BROADBENT. I did really. I wish you had taken half as much interest in me.

NORA. Oh, I was dying to see you, of course. I daresay you can imagine the sensation an Englishman like you would make among us poor Irish people.

BROADBENT. Ah, now you're chaffing me, Miss Reilly: you know you are. You mustn't chaff me. I'm very much in earnest about Ireland and everything Irish. I'm very much in earnest about you and about Larry.

NORA. Larry has nothing to do with me, Mr Broadbent.

BROADBENT. If I really thought that, Miss Reilly, I should—well, I should let myself feel that charm of which I spoke just now more deeply than I—than I—

NORA. Is it making love to me you are?

BROADBENT [scared and much upset]. On my word I believe I am, Miss Reilly. If you say that to me again I shan't answer for myself: all the harps of Ireland are in your voice. [She laughs at him. He suddenly loses his head and seizes her arms, to her great indignation]. Stop laughing: do you hear? I am in earnest— in English earnest. When I say a thing like that to a woman, I mean it. [Releasing her and trying to recover his ordinary manner in spite of his bewildering emotion] I beg your pardon.

NORA. How dare you touch me?

BROADBENT. There are not many things I would not dare for you. That does not sound right perhaps; but I really—[he stops and passes his hand over his forehead, rather lost].

NORA. I think you ought to be ashamed. I think if you were a gentleman, and me alone with you in this place at night, you would die rather than do such a thing.

BROADBENT. You mean that it's an act of treachery to Larry?

NORA. Deed I don't. What has Larry to do with it? It's an act of disrespect and rudeness to me: it shows what you take me for. You can go your way now; and I'll go mine. Goodnight, Mr Broadbent.

BROADBENT. No, please, Miss Reilly. One moment. Listen to me. I'm serious: I'm desperately serious. Tell me that I'm interfering with Larry; and I'll go straight from this spot back to London and never see you again. That's on my honor: I will. Am I interfering with him?

NORA [answering in spite of herself in a sudden spring of bitterness]. I should think you ought to know better than me whether you're interfering with

him. You've seen him oftener than I have. You know him better than I do, by
this time. You've come to me quicker than he has, haven't you?

BROADBENT. I'm bound to tell you, Miss Reilly, that Larry has not
arrived in Rosscullen yet. He meant to get here before me; but his car broke
down; and he may not arrive until to-morrow.

NORA [her face lighting up]. Is that the truth?

BROADBENT. Yes: that's the truth. [She gives a sigh of relief]. You're glad
of that?

NORA [up in arms at once]. Glad indeed! Why should I be glad? As we've
waited eighteen years for him we can afford to wait a day longer, I should think.

BROADBENT. If you really feel like that about him, there may be a chance
for another man yet. Eh?

NORA [deeply offended]. I suppose people are different in England, Mr
Broadbent; so perhaps you don't mean any harm. In Ireland nobody'd mind
what a man'd say in fun, nor take advantage of what a woman might say in
answer to it. If a woman couldn't talk to a man for two minutes at their first
meeting without being treated the way you're treating me, no decent woman
would ever talk to a man at all.

BROADBENT. I don't understand that. I don't admit that. I am sincere;
and my intentions are perfectly honorable. I think you will accept the fact that
I'm an Englishman as a guarantee that I am not a man to act hastily or
romantically, though I confess that your voice had such an extraordinary effect
on me just now when you asked me so quaintly whether I was making love to
you—

NORA [flushing] I never thought—

BROADHHNT [quickly]. Of course you didn't. I'm not so stupid as that.
But I couldn't bear your laughing at the feeling it gave me. You—[again
struggling with a surge of emotion] you don't know what I— [he chokes for a
moment and then blurts out with unnatural steadiness] Will you be my wife?

NORA [promptly]. Deed I won't. The idea! [Looking at him more carefully]
Arra, come home, Mr Broadbent; and get your senses back again. I think you're
not accustomed to potcheen punch in the evening after your tea.

BROADBENT [horrified]. Do you mean to say that I—I—I—my God!
that I appear drunk to you, Miss Reilly?

NORA [compassionately]. How many tumblers had you?

BROADBENT [helplessly]. Two.

NORA. The flavor of the turf prevented you noticing the strength of it.
You'd better come home to bed.

BROADBENT [fearfully agitated]. But this is such a horrible doubt to put
into my mind—to—to—For Heaven's sake, Miss Reilly, am I really drunk?

NORA [soothingly]. You'll be able to judge better in the morning. Come on
now back with me, an think no more about it. [She takes his arm with motherly
solicitude and urges him gently toward the path].

BROADBENT [yielding in despair]. I must be drunk—frightfully drunk; for
your voice drove me out of my senses [he stumbles over a stone]. No: on my

word, on my most sacred word of honor, Miss Reilly, I tripped over that stone. It was an accident; it was indeed.

NORA. Yes, of course it was. Just take my arm, Mr Broadbent, while we're goin down the path to the road. You'll be all right then.

BROADBENT [submissively taking it]. I can't sufficiently apologize, Miss Reilly, or express my sense of your kindness when I am in such a disgusting state. How could I be such a bea— [he trips again] damn the heather! my foot caught in it.

NORA. Steady now, steady. Come along: come. [He is led down to the road in the character of a convicted drunkard. To him there it something divine in the sympathetic indulgence she substitutes for the angry disgust with which one of his own countrywomen would resent his supposed condition. And he has no suspicion of the fact, or of her ignorance of it, that when an Englishman is sentimental he behaves very much as an Irishman does when he is drunk].

ACT III

NEXT morning Broadbent and Larry are sitting at the ends of a breakfast table in the middle of a small grass plot before Cornelius Doyle's house. They have finished their meal, and are buried in newspapers. Most of the crockery is crowded upon a large square black tray of japanned metal. The teapot is of brown delft ware. There is no silver; and the butter, on a dinner plate, is en bloc. The background to this breakfast is the house, a small white slated building, accessible by a half-glazed door. A person coming out into the garden by this door would find the table straight in front of him, and a gate leading to the road half way down the garden on his right; or, if he turned sharp to his left, he could pass round the end of the house through an unkempt shrubbery. The mutilated remnant of a huge planter statue, nearly dissolved by the rains of a century, and vaguely resembling a majestic female in Roman draperies, with a wreath in her hand, stands neglected amid the laurels. Such statues, though apparently works of art, grow naturally in Irish gardens. Their germination is a mystery to the oldest inhabitants, to whose means and taste they are totally foreign.

There is a rustic bench, much roiled by the birds, and decorticated and split by the weather, near the little gate. At the opposite side, a basket lies unmolested because it might as well be there as anywhere else. An empty chair at the table was lately occupied by Cornelius, who has finished his breakfast and gone in to the room in which he receives rents and keeps his books and cash, known in the household as "the office." This chair, like the two occupied by Larry and Broadbent, has a mahogany frame and is upholstered in black horsehair.

Larry rises and goes off through the shrubbery with his newspaper. Hodson comes in through the garden gate, disconsolate. Broadbent, who sits facing the gate, augurs the worst from his expression.

BROADBENT. Have you been to the village?

HODSON. No use, sir. We'll have to get everything from London by parcel post.

BROADBENT. I hope they made you comfortable last night.

HODSON. I was no worse than you were on that sofa, sir. One expects to rough it here, sir.

BROADBENT. We shall have to look out for some other arrangement. [Cheering up irrepressibly] Still, it's no end of a joke. How do you like the Irish, Hodson?

HODSON. Well, sir, they're all right anywhere but in their own country. I've known lots of em in England, and generally liked em. But here, sir, I seem simply to hate em. The feeling come over me the moment we landed at Cork, sir. It's no use my pretendin, sir: I can't bear em. My mind rises up agin their ways, somehow: they rub me the wrong way all over.

BROADBENT. Oh, their faults are on the surface: at heart they are one of the finest races on earth. [Hodson turns away, without affecting to respond to his enthusiasm]. By the way, Hodson—

HODSON [turning]. Yes, sir.

BROADBENT. Did you notice anything about me last night when I came in with that lady?

HODSON [surprised]. No, sir.

BROADBENT. Not any—er—? You may speak frankly.

HODSON. I didn't notice nothing, sir. What sort of thing ded you mean, sir?

BROADBENT. Well—er—er—well, to put it plainly, was I drunk?

HODSON [amazed]. No, sir.

BROADBENT. Quite sure?

HODSON. Well, I should a said rather the opposite, sir. Usually when you've been enjoying yourself, you're a bit hearty like. Last night you seemed rather low, if anything.

BROADBENT. I certainly have no headache. Did you try the pottine, Hodson?

HODSON. I just took a mouthful, sir. It tasted of peat: oh! something horrid, sir. The people here call peat turf. Potcheen and strong porter is what they like, sir. I'm sure I don't know how they can stand it. Give me beer, I say.

BROADBENT. By the way, you told me I couldn't have porridge for breakfast; but Mr Doyle had some.

HODSON. Yes, sir. Very sorry, sir. They call it stirabout, sir: that's how it was. They know no better, sir.

BROADBENT. All right: I'll have some tomorrow.

Hodson goes to the house. When he opens the door he finds Nora and Aunt Judy on the threshold. He stands aside to let them pass, with the air of a well trained servant oppressed by heavy trials. Then he goes in. Broadbent rises. Aunt Judy goes to the table and collects the plates and cups on the tray. Nora goes to the back of the rustic seat and looks out at the gate with the air of a woman accustomed to have nothing to do. Larry returns from the shrubbery.

BROADBENT. Good morning, Miss Doyle.

AUNT JUDY [thinking it absurdly late in the day for such a salutation]. Oh, good morning. [Before moving his plate] Have you done?

BROADBENT. Quite, thank you. You must excuse us for not waiting for you. The country air tempted us to get up early.

AUNT JUDY. N d'ye call this airly, God help you?

LARRY. Aunt Judy probably breakfasted about half past six.

AUNT JUDY. Whisht, you!—draggin the parlor chairs out into the gardn n givin Mr Broadbent his death over his meals out here in the cold air. [To Broadbent] Why d'ye put up with his foolishness, Mr Broadbent?

BROADBENT. I assure you I like the open air.

AUNT JUDY. Ah galong! How can you like what's not natural? I hope you slept well.

NORA. Did anything wake yup with a thump at three o'clock? I thought the house was falling. But then I'm a very light sleeper.

LARRY. I seem to recollect that one of the legs of the sofa in the parlor had a way of coming out unexpectedly eighteen years ago. Was that it, Tom?

BROADBENT [hastily]. Oh, it doesn't matter: I was not hurt—at least—er—

AUNT JUDY. Oh now what a shame! An I told Patsy Farrll to put a nail in it.

BROADBENT. He did, Miss Doyle. There was a nail, certainly.

AUNT JUDY. Dear oh dear!

An oldish peasant farmer, small, leathery, peat faced, with a deep voice and a surliness that is meant to be aggressive, and is in effect pathetic—the voice of a man of hard life and many sorrows—comes in at the gate. He is old enough to have perhaps worn a long tailed frieze coat and knee breeches in his time; but now he is dressed respectably in a black frock coat, tall hat, and pollard colored trousers; and his face is as clean as washing can make it, though that is not saying much, as the habit is recently acquired and not yet congenial.

THE NEW-COMER [at the gate]. God save all here! [He comes a little way into the garden].

LARRY [patronizingly, speaking across the garden to him]. Is that yourself, Mat Haffigan? Do you remember me?

MATTHEW [intentionally rude and blunt]. No. Who are you?

NORA. Oh, I'm sure you remember him, Mr Haffigan.

MATTHEW [grudgingly admitting it]. I suppose he'll be young Larry Doyle that was.

LARRY. Yes.

MATTHEW [to Larry]. I hear you done well in America.

LARRY. Fairly well.

MATTHEW. I suppose you saw me brother Andy out dhere.

LARRY. No. It's such a big place that looking for a man there is like looking for a needle in a bundle of hay. They tell me he's a great man out there.

MATTHEW. So he is, God be praised. Where's your father?

AUNT JUDY. He's inside, in the office, Mr Haffigan, with Barney Doarn n Father Dempsey.

Matthew, without wasting further words on the company, goes curtly into the house.

LARRY [staring after him]. Is anything wrong with old Mat?

NORA. No. He's the same as ever. Why?

LARRY. He's not the same to me. He used to be very civil to Master Larry: a deal too civil, I used to think. Now he's as surly and stand-off as a bear.

AUNT JUDY. Oh sure he's bought his farm in the Land Purchase. He's independent now.

NORA. It's made a great change, Larry. You'd harly know the old tenants now. You'd think it was a liberty to speak t'dhem—some o dhem. [She goes to the table, and helps to take off the cloth, which she and Aunt Judy fold up between them].

AUNT JUDY. I wonder what he wants to see Corny for. He hasn't been here since he paid the last of his old rent; and then he as good as threw it in Corny's face, I thought.

LARRY. No wonder! Of course they all hated us like the devil. Ugh! [Moodily] I've seen them in that office, telling my father what a fine boy I was, and plastering him with compliments, with your honor here and your honor there, when all the time their fingers were itching to beat his throat.

AUNT JUDY. Deedn why should they want to hurt poor Corny? It was he that got Mat the lease of his farm, and stood up for him as an industrious decent man.

BROADBENT. Was he industrious? That's remarkable, you know, in an Irishman.

LARRY. Industrious! That man's industry used to make me sick, even as a boy. I tell you, an Irish peasant's industry is not human: it's worse than the industry of a coral insect. An Englishman has some sense about working: he never does more than he can help—and hard enough to get him to do that without scamping it; but an Irishman will work as if he'd die the moment he stopped. That man Matthew Haffigan and his brother Andy made a farm out of a patch of stones on the hillside—cleared it and dug it with their own naked hands and bought their first spade out of their first crop of potatoes. Talk of making two blades of wheat grow where one grew before! those two men made a whole field of wheat grow where not even a furze bush had ever got its head up between the stones.

BROADBENT. That was magnificent, you know. Only a great race is capable of producing such men.

LARRY. Such fools, you mean! What good was it to them? The moment they'd done it, the landlord put a rent of 5 pounds a year on them, and turned them out because they couldn't pay it.

AUNT JUDY. Why couldn't they pay as well as Billy Byrne that took it after them?

LARRY [angrily]. You know very well that Billy Byrne never paid it. He only offered it to get possession. He never paid it.

AUNT JUDY. That was because Andy Haffigan hurt him with a brick so that he was never the same again. Andy had to run away to America for it.

BROADBENT [glowing with indignation]. Who can blame him, Miss Doyle? Who can blame him?

LARRY [impatiently]. Oh, rubbish! What's the good of the man that's starved out of a farm murdering the man that's starved into it? Would you have done such a thing?

BROADBENT. Yes. I—I—I—I—[stammering with fury] I should have shot the confounded landlord, and wrung the neck of the damned agent, and blown the farm up with dynamite, and Dublin Castle along with it.

LARRY. Oh yes: you'd have done great things; and a fat lot of good you'd have got out of it, too! That's an Englishman all over! make bad laws and give away all the land, and then, when your economic incompetence produces its natural and inevitable results, get virtuously indignant and kill the people that carry out your laws.

AUNT JUDY. Sure never mind him, Mr Broadbent. It doesn't matter, anyhow, because there's harly any landlords left; and ther'll soon be none at all.

LARRY. On the contrary, ther'll soon be nothing else; and the Lord help Ireland then!

AUNT JUDY. Ah, you're never satisfied, Larry. [To Nora] Come on, alanna, an make the paste for the pie. We can leave them to their talk. They don't want us [she takes up the tray and goes into the house].

BROADBENT [rising and gallantly protesting] Oh, Miss Doyle! Really, really—

Nora, following Aunt Judy with the rolled-up cloth in her hands, looks at him and strikes him dumb. He watches her until she disappears; then comes to Larry and addresses him with sudden intensity.

BROADBENT. Larry.

LARRY. What is it?

BROADBENT. I got drunk last night, and proposed to Miss Reilly.

LARRY. You HWAT??? [He screams with laughter in the falsetto Irish register unused for that purpose in England].

BROADBENT. What are you laughing at?

LARRY [stopping dead]. I don't know. That's the sort of thing an Irishman laughs at. Has she accepted you?

BROADBENT. I shall never forget that with the chivalry of her nation, though I was utterly at her mercy, she refused me.

LARRY. That was extremely improvident of her. [Beginning to reflect] But look here: when were you drunk? You were sober enough when you came back from the Round Tower with her.

BROADBENT. No, Larry, I was drunk, I am sorry to say. I had two tumblers of punch. She had to lead me home. You must have noticed it.

LARRY. I did not.

BROADBENT. She did.

LARRY. May I ask how long it took you to come to business? You can hardly have known her for more than a couple of hours.

BROADBENT. I am afraid it was hardly a couple of minutes. She was not here when I arrived; and I saw her for the first time at the tower.

LARRY. Well, you are a nice infant to be let loose in this country! Fancy the potcheen going to your head like that!

BROADBENT. Not to my head, I think. I have no headache; and I could speak distinctly. No: potcheen goes to the heart, not to the head. What ought I to do?

LARRY. Nothing. What need you do?

BROADBENT. There is rather a delicate moral question involved. The point is, was I drunk enough not to be morally responsible for my proposal? Or was I sober enough to be bound to repeat it now that I am undoubtedly sober?

LARRY. I should see a little more of her before deciding.

BROADBENT. No, no. That would not be right. That would not be fair. I am either under a moral obligation or I am not. I wish I knew how drunk I was.

LARRY. Well, you were evidently in a state of blithering sentimentality, anyhow.

BROADBENT. That is true, Larry: I admit it. Her voice has a most extraordinary effect on me. That Irish voice!

LARRY [sympathetically]. Yes, I know. When I first went to London I very nearly proposed to walk out with a waitress in an Aerated Bread shop because her Whitechapel accent was so distinguished, so quaintly touching, so pretty—

BROADBENT [angrily]. Miss Reilly is not a waitress, is she?

LARRY. Oh, come! The waitress was a very nice girl.

BROADBENT. You think every Englishwoman an angel. You really have coarse tastes in that way, Larry. Miss Reilly is one of the finer types: a type rare in England, except perhaps in the best of the aristocracy.

LARRY. Aristocracy be blowed! Do you know what Nora eats?

BROADBENT. Eats! what do you mean?

LARRY. Breakfast: tea and bread-and-butter, with an occasional rasher, and an egg on special occasions: say on her birthday. Dinner in the middle of the day, one course and nothing else. In the evening, tea and bread-and-butter again. You compare her with your Englishwomen who wolf down from three to five meat meals a day; and naturally you find her a sylph. The difference is not a difference of type: it's the difference between the woman who eats not wisely but too well, and the woman who eats not wisely but too little.

BROADBENT [furious]. Larry: you—you—you disgust me. You are a damned fool. [He sits down angrily on the rustic seat, which sustains the shock with difficulty].

LARRY. Steady! stead-eee! [He laughs and seats himself on the table].

Cornelius Doyle, Father Dempsey, Barney Doran, and Matthew Haffigan come from the house. Doran is a stout bodied, short armed, roundheaded, red-haired man on the verge of middle age, of sanguine temperament, with an enormous capacity for derisive, obscene, blasphemous, or merely cruel and senseless fun, and a violent and impetuous intolerance of other temperaments and other opinions, all this representing energy and capacity wasted and demoralized by want of sufficient training and social pressure to force it into beneficent activity and build a character with it; for Barney is by no means either stupid or weak. He is recklessly untidy as to his person; but the worst effects of his neglect are mitigated by a powdering of flour and mill dust; and his unbrushed clothes, made of a fashionable tailor's sackcloth, were evidently chosen regardless of expense for the sake of their appearance.

Matthew Haffigan, ill at ease, coasts the garden shyly on the shrubbery side until he anchors near the basket, where he feels least in the way. The priest comes to the table and slaps Larry on the shoulder. Larry, turning quickly, and recognizing Father Dempsey, alights from the table and shakes the priest's hand warmly. Doran comes down the garden between Father Dempsey and Matt; and Cornelius, on the other side of the table, turns to Broadbent, who rises genially.

CORNELIUS. I think we all met las night.

DORAN. I hadn't that pleasure.

CORNELIUS. To be sure, Barney: I forgot. [To Broadbent, introducing

Barney] Mr Doran. He owns that fine mill you noticed from the car.

BROADBENT [delighted with them all]. Most happy, Mr Doran. Very pleased indeed.

Doran, not quite sure whether he is being courted or patronized, nods independently.

DORAN. How's yourself, Larry?

LARRY. Finely, thank you. No need to ask you. [Doran grins; and they shake hands].

CORNELIUS. Give Father Dempsey a chair, Larry.

Matthew Haffigan runs to the nearest end of the table and takes the chair from it, placing it near the basket; but Larry has already taken the chair from the other end and placed it in front of the table. Father Dempsey accepts that more central position.

CORNELIUS. Sit down, Barney, will you; and you, Mat.

Doran takes the chair Mat is still offering to the priest; and poor Matthew, outfaced by the miller, humbly turns the basket upside down and sits on it. Cornelius brings his own breakfast chair from the table and sits down on Father Dempsey's right. Broadbent resumes his seat on the rustic bench. Larry crosses to the bench and is about to sit down beside him when Broadbent holds him off nervously.

BROADBENT. Do you think it will bear two, Larry?

LARRY. Perhaps not. Don't move. I'll stand. [He posts himself behind the bench].

They are all now seated, except Larry; and the session assumes a portentous air, as if something important were coming.

CORNELIUS. Props you'll explain, Father Dempsey.

FATHER DEMPSEY. No, no: go on, you: the Church has no politics.

CORNELIUS. Were yever thinkin o goin into parliament at all, Larry?

LARRY. Me!

FATHER DEMPSEY [encouragingly] Yes, you. Hwy not?

LARRY. I'm afraid my ideas would not be popular enough.

CORNELIUS. I don't know that. Do you, Barney?

DORAN. There's too much blatherumskite in Irish politics a dale too much.

LARRY. But what about your present member? Is he going to retire?

CORNELIUS. No: I don't know that he is.

LARRY [interrogatively]. Well? then?

MATTHEW [breaking out with surly bitterness]. We've had enough of his foolish talk agen lanlords. Hwat call has he to talk about the lan, that never was outside of a city office in his life?

CORNELIUS. We're tired of him. He doesn't know hwere to stop. Every man can't own land; and some men must own it to employ them. It was all very well when solid men like Doran and me and Mat were kep from ownin land. But hwat man in his senses ever wanted to give land to Patsy Farrll an dhe like o him?

BROADBENT. But surely Irish landlordism was accountable for what Mr Haffigan suffered.

MATTHEW. Never mind hwat I suffered. I know what I suffered adhout you tellin me. But did I ever ask for more dhan the farm I made wid me own hans: tell me that, Corny Doyle, and you that knows. Was I fit for the responsibility or was I not? [Snarling angrily at Cornelius] Am I to be compared to Patsy Farrll, that doesn't harly know his right hand from his left? What did he ever suffer, I'd like to know?

CORNELIUS. That's just what I say. I wasn't comparin you to your disadvantage.

MATTHEW [implacable]. Then hwat did you mane be talkin about givin him lan?

DORAN. Aisy, Mat, aisy. You're like a bear with a sore back.

MATTHEW [trembling with rage]. An who are you, to offer to taitch me manners?

FATHER DEMPSEY [admonitorily]. Now, now, now, Mat none o dhat. How often have I told you you're too ready to take offence where none is meant? You don't understand: Corny Doyle is saying just what you want to have said. [To Cornelius] Go on, Mr Doyle; and never mind him.

MATTHEW [rising]. Well, if me lan is to be given to Patsy and his like, I'm goin oura dhis. I—

DORAN [with violent impatience] Arra who's goin to give your lan to Patsy, yowl fool ye?

FATHER DEMPSEY. Aisy, Barney, aisy. [Sternly, to Mat] I told you, Matthew Haffigan, that Corny Doyle was sayin nothin against you. I'm sorry your priest's word is not good enough for you. I'll go, sooner than stay to make you commit a sin against the Church. Good morning, gentlemen. [He rises. They all rise, except Broadbent].

DORAN [to Mat]. There! Sarve you dam well right, you cantankerous oul noodle.

MATTHEW [appalled]. Don't say dhat, Fadher Dempsey. I never had a thought agen you or the Holy Church. I know I'm a bit hasty when I think about the lan. I ax your pardn for it.

FATHER DEMPSEY [resuming his seat with dignified reserve]. Very well: I'll overlook it this time. [He sits down. The others sit down, except Matthew. Father Dempsey, about to ask Corny to proceed, remembers Matthew and turns to him, giving him just a crumb of graciousness]. Sit down, Mat. [Matthew, crushed, sits down in disgrace, and is silent, his eyes shifting piteously from one speaker to another in an intensely mistrustful effort to understand them]. Go on, Mr Doyle. We can make allowances. Go on.

CORNELIUS. Well, you see how it is, Larry. Round about here, we've got the land at last; and we want no more Goverment meddlin. We want a new class o man in parliament: one dhat knows dhat the farmer's the real backbone o the country, n doesn't care a snap of his fingers for the shoutn o the riff-raff in the towns, or for the foolishness of the laborers.

DORAN. Aye; an dhat can afford to live in London and pay his own way until Home Rule comes, instead o wantin subscriptions and the like.

FATHER DEMPSEY. Yes: that's a good point, Barney. When too much money goes to politics, it's the Church that has to starve for it. A member of parliament ought to be a help to the Church instead of a burden on it.

LARRY. Here's a chance for you, Tom. What do you say?

BROADBENT [deprecatory, but important and smiling]. Oh, I have no claim whatever to the seat. Besides, I'm a Saxon.

DORAN. A hwat?

BROADBENT. A Saxon. An Englishman.

DORAN. An Englishman. Bedad I never heard it called dhat before.

MATTHEW [cunningly]. If I might make so bould, Fadher, I wouldn't say but an English Prodestn mightn't have a more indepindent mind about the lan, an be less afeerd to spake out about it, dhan an Irish Catholic.

CORNELIUS. But sure Larry's as good as English: aren't you, Larry?

LARRY. You may put me out of your head, father, once for all.

CORNELIUS. Arra why?

LARRY. I have strong opinions which wouldn't suit you.

DORAN [rallying him blatantly]. Is it still Larry the bould Fenian?

LARRY. No: the bold Fenian is now an older and possibly foolisher man.

CORNELIUS. Hwat does it matter to us hwat your opinions are? You know that your father's bought his farm, just the same as Mat here n Barney's mill. All we ask now is to be let alone. You've nothin against that, have you?

LARRY. Certainly I have. I don't believe in letting anybody or anything alone.

CORNELIUS [losing his temper]. Arra what d'ye mean, you young fool? Here I've got you the offer of a good seat in parliament; n you think yourself mighty smart to stand there and talk foolishness to me. Will you take it or leave it?

LARRY. Very well: I'll take it with pleasure if you'll give it to me.

CORNELIUS [subsiding sulkily]. Well, why couldn't you say so at once? It's a good job you've made up your mind at last.

DORAN [suspiciously]. Stop a bit, stop a bit.

MATTHEW [writhing between his dissatisfaction and his fear of the priest]. It's not because he's your son that he's to get the sate. Fadher Dempsey: wouldn't you think well to ask him what he manes about the lan?

LARRY [coming down on Mat promptly]. I'll tell you, Mat. I always thought it was a stupid, lazy, good-for-nothing sort of thing to leave the land in the hands of the old landlords without calling them to a strict account for the use they made of it, and the condition of the people on it. I could see for myself that they thought of nothing but what they could get out of it to spend in England; and that they mortgaged and mortgaged until hardly one of them owned his own property or could have afforded to keep it up decently if he'd wanted to. But I tell you plump and plain, Mat, that if anybody thinks things will be any better now that the land is handed over to a lot of little men like you, without calling you to account either, they're mistaken.

MATTHEW [sullenly]. What call have you to look down on me? I suppose you think you're everybody because your father was a land agent.

LARRY. What call have you to look down on Patsy Farrell? I suppose you think you're everybody because you own a few fields.

MATTHEW. Was Patsy Farrll ever ill used as I was ill used? tell me dhat.

LARRY. He will be, if ever he gets into your power as you were in the power of your old landlord. Do you think, because you're poor and ignorant and half-crazy with toiling and moiling morning noon and night, that you'll be any less greedy and oppressive to them that have no land at all than old Nick Lestrange, who was an educated travelled gentleman that would not have been tempted as hard by a hundred pounds as you'd be by five shillings? Nick was too high above Patsy Farrell to be jealous of him; but you, that are only one little step above him, would die sooner than let him come up that step; and well you know it.

MATTHEW [black with rage, in a low growl]. Lemme oura this. [He tries to rise; but Doran catches his coat and drags him down again] I'm goin, I say. [Raising his voice] Leggo me coat, Barney Doran.

DORAN. Sit down, yowl omadhaun, you. [Whispering] Don't you want to stay an vote against him?

FATHER DEMPSEY [holding up his finger] Mat! [Mat subsides]. Now, now, now! come, come! Hwats all dhis about Patsy Farrll? Hwy need you fall out about HIM?

LARRY. Because it was by using Patsy's poverty to undersell England in the markets of the world that we drove England to ruin Ireland. And she'll ruin us again the moment we lift our heads from the dust if we trade in cheap labor; and serve us right too! If I get into parliament, I'll try to get an Act to prevent any of you from giving Patsy less than a pound a week [they all start, hardly able to believe their ears] or working him harder than you'd work a horse that cost you fifty guineas.

DORAN. Hwat!!!

CORNELIUS [aghast]. A pound a—God save us! the boy's mad.

Matthew, feeling that here is something quite beyond his powers, turns openmouthed to the priest, as if looking for nothing less than the summary excommunication of Larry.

LARRY. How is the man to marry and live a decent life on less?

FATHER DEMPSEY. Man alive, hwere have you been living all these years? and hwat have you been dreaming of? Why, some o dhese honest men here can't make that much out o the land for themselves, much less give it to a laborer.

LARRY [now thoroughly roused]. Then let them make room for those who can. Is Ireland never to have a chance? First she was given to the rich; and now that they have gorged on her flesh, her bones are to be flung to the poor, that can do nothing but suck the marrow out of her. If we can't have men of honor own the land, lets have men of ability. If we can't have men with ability, let us at least have men with capital. Anybody's better than Mat, who has neither honor, nor ability, nor capital, nor anything but mere brute labor and greed in him, Heaven help him!

DORAN. Well, we're not all foostherin oul doddherers like Mat. [Pleasantly, to the subject of this description] Are we, Mat?

LARRY. For modern industrial purposes you might just as well be, Barney. You're all children: the big world that I belong to has gone past you and left you. Anyhow, we Irishmen were never made to be farmers; and we'll never do any good at it. We're like the Jews: the Almighty gave us brains, and bid us farm them, and leave the clay and the worms alone.

FATHER DEMPSEY [with gentle irony]. Oh! is it Jews you want to make of us? I must catechize you a bit meself, I think. The next thing you'll be proposing is to repeal the disestablishment of the so-called Irish Church.

LARRY. Yes: why not? [Sensation].

MATTHEW [rancorously]. He's a turncoat.

LARRY. St Peter, the rock on which our Church was built, was crucified head downwards for being a turncoat.

FATHER DEMPSEY [with a quiet authoritative dignity which checks Doran, who is on the point of breaking out]. That's true. You hold your tongue as befits your ignorance, Matthew Haffigan; and trust your priest to deal with this young man. Now, Larry Doyle, whatever the blessed St Peter was crucified for, it was not for being a Prodestan. Are you one?

LARRY. No. I am a Catholic intelligent enough to see that the Protestants are never more dangerous to us than when they are free from all alliances with the State. The so-called Irish Church is stronger today than ever it was.

MATTHEW. Fadher Dempsey: will you tell him dhat me mother's ant was shot and kilt dead in the sthreet o Rosscullen be a soljer in the tithe war? [Frantically] He wants to put the tithes on us again. He—

LARRY [interrupting him with overbearing contempt]. Put the tithes on you again! Did the tithes ever come off you? Was your land any dearer when you paid the tithe to the parson than it was when you paid the same money to Nick Lestrange as rent, and he handed it over to the Church Sustentation Fund? Will you always be duped by Acts of Parliament that change nothing but the necktie of the man that picks your pocket? I'll tell you what I'd do with you, Mat Haffigan: I'd make you pay tithes to your own Church. I want the Catholic Church established in Ireland: that's what I want. Do you think that I, brought up to regard myself as the son of a great and holy Church, can bear to see her begging her bread from the ignorance and superstition of men like you? I would have her as high above worldly want as I would have her above worldly pride or ambition. Aye; and I would have Ireland compete with Rome itself for the chair of St Peter and the citadel of the Church; for Rome, in spite of all the blood of the martyrs, is pagan at heart to this day, while in Ireland the people is the Church and the Church the people.

FATHER DEMPSEY [startled, but not at all displeased]. Whisht, man! You're worse than mad Pether Keegan himself.

BROADBENT [who has listened in the greatest astonishment]. You amaze me, Larry. Who would have thought of your coming out like this! [Solemnly] But much as I appreciate your really brilliant eloquence, I implore you not to desert the great Liberal principle of Disestablishment.

LARRY. I am not a Liberal: Heaven forbid! A disestablished Church is the worst tyranny a nation can groan under.

BROADBENT [making a wry face]. DON'T be paradoxical, Larry. It really gives me a pain in my stomach.

LARRY. You'll soon find out the truth of it here. Look at Father Dempsey! he is disestablished: he has nothing to hope or fear from the State; and the result is that he's the most powerful man in Rosscullen. The member for Rosscullen would shake in his shoes if Father Dempsey looked crooked at him. [Father Dempsey smiles, by no means averse to this acknowledgment of his authority]. Look at yourself! you would defy the established Archbishop of Canterbury ten times a day; but catch you daring to say a word that would shock a Nonconformist! not you. The Conservative party today is the only one that's not priestridden—excuse the expression, Father [Father Dempsey nods tolerantly]— cause it's the only one that has established its Church and can prevent a clergyman becoming a bishop if he's not a Statesman as well as a Churchman.

He stops. They stare at him dumbfounded, and leave it to the priest to answer him.

FATHER DEMPSEY [judicially]. Young man: you'll not be the member for Rosscullen; but there's more in your head than the comb will take out.

LARRY. I'm sorry to disappoint you, father; but I told you it would be no use. And now I think the candidate had better retire and leave you to discuss his successor. [He takes a newspaper from the table and goes away through the shrubbery amid dead silence, all turning to watch him until he passes out of sight round the corner of the house].

DORAN [dazed]. Hwat sort of a fella is he at all at all?

FATHER DEMPSEY. He's a clever lad: there's the making of a man in him yet.

MATTHEW [in consternation]. D'ye mane to say dhat yll put him into parliament to bring back Nick Lesthrange on me, and to put tithes on me, and to rob me for the like o Patsy Farrll, because he's Corny Doyle's only son?

DORAN [brutally]. Arra hould your whisht: who's goin to send him into parliament? Maybe you'd like us to send you dhere to thrate them to a little o your anxiety about dhat dirty little podato patch o yours.

MATTHEW [plaintively]. Am I to be towld dhis afther all me sufferins?

DORAN. Och, I'm tired o your sufferins. We've been hearin nothin else ever since we was childher but sufferins. Haven it wasn't yours it was somebody else's; and haven it was nobody else's it was ould Irelan's. How the divil are we to live on wan anodher's sufferins?

FATHER DEMPSEY. That's a thrue word, Barney Doarn; only your tongue's a little too familiar wi dhe devil. [To Mat] If you'd think a little more o the sufferins of the blessed saints, Mat, an a little less o your own, you'd find the way shorter from your farm to heaven. [Mat is about to reply] Dhere now! Dhat's enough! we know you mean well; an I'm not angry with you.

BROADBENT. Surely, Mr Haffigan, you can see the simple explanation of all this. My friend Larry Doyle is a most brilliant speaker; but he's a Tory: an ingrained oldfashioned Tory.

CORNELIUS. N how d'ye make dhat out, if I might ask you, Mr Broadbent?

BROADBENT [collecting himself for a political deliverance]. Well, you know, Mr Doyle, there's a strong dash of Toryism in the Irish character. Larry himself says that the great Duke of Wellington was the most typical Irishman that ever lived. Of course that's an absurd paradox; but still there's a great deal of truth in it. Now I am a Liberal. You know the great principles of the Liberal party. Peace—

FATHER DEMPSEY [piously]. Hear! hear!

BROADBENT [encouraged]. Thank you. Retrenchment—[he waits for further applause].

MATTHEW [timidly]. What might rethrenchment mane now?

BROADBENT. It means an immense reduction in the burden of the rates and taxes.

MATTHEW [respectfully approving]. Dhats right. Dhats right, sir.

BROADBENT [perfunctorily]. And, of course, Reform.

CORNELIUS   }
FATHER DEMPSEY} [conventionally]. Of course.
DORAN   }

MATTHEW [still suspicious]. Hwat does Reform mane, sir? Does it mane altherin annythin dhats as it is now?

BROADBENT [impressively]. It means, Mr Haffigan, maintaining those reforms which have already been conferred on humanity by the Liberal Party, and trusting for future developments to the free activity of a free people on the basis of those reforms.

DORAN. Dhat's right. No more meddlin. We're all right now: all we want is to be let alone.

CORNELIUS. Hwat about Home Rule?

BROADBENT [rising so as to address them more imposingly]. I really cannot tell you what I feel about Home Rule without using the language of hyperbole.

DORAN. Savin Fadher Dempsey's presence, eh?

BROADBENT [not understanding him] Quite so—er—oh yes. All I can say is that as an Englishman I blush for the Union. It is the blackest stain on our national history. I look forward to the time-and it cannot be far distant, gentlemen, because Humanity is looking forward to it too, and insisting on it with no uncertain voice—I look forward to the time when an Irish legislature shall arise once more on the emerald pasture of College Green, and the Union Jack—that detestable symbol of a decadent Imperialism—be replaced by a flag as green as the island over which it waves—a flag on which we shall ask for

England only a modest quartering in memory of our great party and of the immortal name of our grand old leader.

DORAN [enthusiastically]. Dhat's the style, begob! [He smites his knee, and winks at Mat].

MATTHEW. More power to you, Sir!

BROADBENT. I shall leave you now, gentlemen, to your deliberations. I should like to have enlarged on the services rendered by the Liberal Party to the religious faith of the great majority of the people of Ireland; but I shall content myself with saying that in my opinion you should choose no representative who—no matter what his personal creed may be—is not an ardent supporter of freedom of conscience, and is not prepared to prove it by contributions, as lavish as his means will allow, to the great and beneficent work which you, Father Dempsey [Father Dempsey bows], are doing for the people of Rosscullen. Nor should the lighter, but still most important question of the sports of the people be forgotten. The local cricket club—

CORNELIUS. The hwat!

DORAN. Nobody plays bats ball here, if dhat's what you mean.

BROADBENT. Well, let us say quoits. I saw two men, I think, last night—but after all, these are questions of detail. The main thing is that your candidate, whoever he may be, shall be a man of some means, able to help the locality instead of burdening it. And if he were a countryman of my own, the moral effect on the House of Commons would be immense! tremendous! Pardon my saying these few words: nobody feels their impertinence more than I do. Good morning, gentlemen.

He turns impressively to the gate, and trots away, congratulating himself,, with a little twist of his head and cock of his eye, on having done a good stroke of political business.

HAFFIGAN [awestruck]. Good morning, sir.

THE REST. Good morning. [They watch him vacantly until he is out of earshot].

CORNELIUS. Hwat d'ye think, Father Dempsey?

FATHER DEMPSEY [indulgently] Well, he hasn't much sense, God help him; but for the matter o that, neither has our present member.

DORAN. Arra musha he's good enough for parliament what is there to do there but gas a bit, an chivy the Goverment, an vote wi dh Irish party?

CORNELIUS [ruminatively]. He's the queerest Englishman I ever met. When he opened the paper dhis mornin the first thing he saw was that an English expedition had been bet in a battle in Inja somewhere; an he was as pleased as Punch! Larry told him that if he'd been alive when the news o Waterloo came, he'd a died o grief over it. Bedad I don't think he's quite right in his head.

DORAN. Divil a matther if he has plenty o money. He'll do for us right enough.

MATTHEW [deeply impressed by Broadbent, and unable to understand their levity concerning him]. Did you mind what he said about rethrenchment?

That was very good, I thought.

FATHER DEMPSEY. You might find out from Larry, Corny, what his means are. God forgive us all! it's poor work spoiling the Egyptians, though we have good warrant for it; so I'd like to know how much spoil there is before I commit meself. [He rises. They all rise respectfully].

CORNELIUS [ruefully]. I'd set me mind on Larry himself for the seat; but I suppose it can't be helped.

FATHER DEMPSEY [consoling him]. Well, the boy's young yet; an he has a head on him. Goodbye, all. [He goes out through the gate].

DORAN. I must be goin, too. [He directs Cornelius's attention to what is passing in the road]. Look at me bould Englishman shakin hans wid Fadher Dempsey for all the world like a candidate on election day. And look at Fadher Dempsey givin him a squeeze an a wink as much as to say It's all right, me boy. You watch him shakin hans with me too: he's waitn for me. I'll tell him he's as good as elected. [He goes, chuckling mischievously].

CORNELIUS. Come in with me, Mat. I think I'll sell you the pig after all. Come in an wet the bargain.

MATTHEW [instantly dropping into the old whine of the tenant]. I'm afeerd I can't afford the price, sir. [He follows Cornelius into the house].

Larry, newspaper still in hand, comes back through the shrubbery. Broadbent returns through the gate.

LARRY. Well? What has happened.

BROADBENT [hugely self-satisfied]. I think I've done the trick this time. I just gave them a bit of straight talk; and it went home. They were greatly impressed: everyone of those men believes in me and will vote for me when the question of selecting a candidate comes up. After all, whatever you say, Larry, they like an Englishman. They feel they can trust him, I suppose.

LARRY. Oh ! they've transferred the honor to you, have they?

BROADBENT [complacently]. Well, it was a pretty obvious move, I should think. You know, these fellows have plenty of shrewdness in spite of their Irish oddity. [Hodson comes from the house. Larry sits in Doran's chair and reads]. Oh, by the way, Hodson—

HODSON [coming between Broadbent and Larry]. Yes, sir?

BROADBENT. I want you to be rather particular as to how you treat the people here.

HODSON. I haven't treated any of em yet, sir. If I was to accept all the treats they offer me I shouldn't be able to stand at this present moment, sir.

BROADBENT. Oh well, don't be too stand-offish, you know, Hodson. I should like you to be popular. If it costs anything I'll make it up to you. It doesn't matter if you get a bit upset at first: they'll like you all the better for it.

HODSON. I'm sure you're very kind, sir; but it don't seem to matter to me whether they like me or not. I'm not going to stand for parliament here, sir.

BROADBENT. Well, I am. Now do you understand?

HODSON [waking up at once]. Oh, I beg your pardon, sir, I'm sure. I understand, sir.

CORNELIUS [appearing at the house door with Mat]. Patsy'll drive the pig over this evenin, Mat. Goodbye. [He goes back into the house. Mat makes for the gate. Broadbent stops him. Hodson, pained by the derelict basket, picks it up and carries it away behind the house].

BROADBENT [beaming candidatorially]. I must thank you very particularly, Mr Haffigan, for your support this morning. I value it because I know that the real heart of a nation is the class you represent, the yeomanry.

MATTHEW [aghast] The yeomanry!!!

LARRY [looking up from his paper]. Take care, Tom! In Rosscullen a yeoman means a sort of Orange Bashi-Bazouk. In England, Mat, they call a freehold farmer a yeoman.

MATTHEW [huffily]. I don't need to be insthructed be you, Larry Doyle. Some people think no one knows anythin but dhemselves. [To Broadbent, deferentially] Of course I know a gentleman like you would not compare me to the yeomanry. Me own granfather was flogged in the sthreets of Athenmullet be them when they put a gun in the thatch of his house an then went and found it there, bad cess to them!

BROADBENT [with sympathetic interest]. Then you are not the first martyr of your family, Mr Haffigan?

MATTHEW. They turned me out o the farm I made out of the stones o Little Rosscullen hill wid me own hans.

BROADBENT. I have heard about it; and my blood still boils at the thought. [Calling] Hodson—

HODSON [behind the corner of the house] Yes, sir. [He hurries forward].

BROADBENT. Hodson: this gentleman's sufferings should make every Englishman think. It is want of thought rather than want of heart that allows such iniquities to disgrace society.

HODSON [prosaically]. Yes sir.

MATTHEW. Well, I'll be goin. Good mornin to you kindly, sir.

BROADBENT. You have some distance to go, Mr Haffigan: will you allow me to drive you home?

MATTHEW. Oh sure it'd be throublin your honor.

BROADBENT. I insist: it will give me the greatest pleasure, I assure you. My car is in the stable: I can get it round in five minutes.

MATTHEW. Well, sir, if you wouldn't mind, we could bring the pig I've just bought from Corny.

BROADBENT [with enthusiasm]. Certainly, Mr Haffigan: it will be quite delightful to drive with a pig in the car: I shall feel quite like an Irishman. Hodson: stay with Mr Haffigan; and give him a hand with the pig if necessary. Come, Larry; and help me. [He rushes away through the shrubbery].

LARRY [throwing the paper ill-humoredly on the chair]. Look here, Tom! here, I say! confound it! [he runs after him].

MATTHEW [glowering disdainfully at Hodson, and sitting down on Cornelius's chair as an act of social self-assertion] N are you the valley?

HODSON. The valley? Oh, I follow you: yes: I'm Mr Broadbent's valet.

MATTHEW. Ye have an aisy time of it: you look purty sleek. [With suppressed ferocity] Look at me! Do I look sleek?

HODSON [sadly]. I wish I ad your ealth: you look as hard as nails. I suffer from an excess of uric acid.

MATTHEW. Musha what sort o disease is zhouragassid? Didjever suffer from injustice and starvation? Dhat's the Irish disease. It's aisy for you to talk o sufferin, an you livin on the fat o the land wid money wrung from us.

HODSON [Coolly]. Wots wrong with you, old chap? Has ennybody been doin ennything to you?

MATTHEW. Anythin timme! Didn't your English masther say that the blood biled in him to hear the way they put a rint on me for the farm I made wid me own hans, and turned me out of it to give it to Billy Byrne?

HODSON. Ow, Tom Broadbent's blood boils pretty easy over ennything that appens out of his own country. Don't you be taken in by my ole man, Paddy.

MATTHEW [indignantly]. Paddy yourself! How dar you call me Paddy?

HODSON [unmoved]. You just keep your hair on and listen to me. You Irish people are too well off: that's what's the matter with you. [With sudden passion] You talk of your rotten little farm because you made it by chuckin a few stownes dahn a hill! Well, wot price my grenfawther, I should like to know, that fitted up a fuss clawss shop and built up a fuss clawss drapery business in London by sixty years work, and then was chucked aht of it on is ed at the end of is lease withaht a penny for his goodwill. You talk of evictions! you that cawn't be moved until you've run up eighteen months rent. I once ran up four weeks in Lambeth when I was aht of a job in winter. They took the door off its inges and the winder aht of its sashes on me, and gave my wife pnoomownia. I'm a widower now. [Between his teeth] Gawd! when I think of the things we Englishmen av to put up with, and hear you Irish hahlin abaht your silly little grievances, and see the way you makes it worse for us by the rotten wages you'll come over and take and the rotten places you'll sleep in, I jast feel that I could take the oul bloomin British awland and make you a present of it, jast to let you find out wot real ardship's like.

MATTHEW [starting up, more in scandalized incredulity than in anger]. D'ye have the face to set up England agen Ireland for injustices an wrongs an disthress an sufferin?

HODSON [with intense disgust and contempt, but with Cockney coolness]. Ow, chuck it, Paddy. Cheese it. You danno wot ardship is over ere: all you know is ah to ahl abaht it. You take the biscuit at that, you do. I'm a Owm Ruler, I am. Do you know why?

MATTHEW [equally contemptuous]. D'ye know, yourself?

HODSON. Yes I do. It's because I want a little attention paid to my own country; and thet'll never be as long as your chaps are ollerin at Wesminister as if nowbody mettered but your own bloomin selves. Send em back to hell or C'naught, as good oul English Cromwell said. I'm jast sick of Ireland. Let it gow. Cut the cable. Make it a present to Germany to keep the oul Kyzer busy for a while; and give poor owld England a chawnce: thets wot I say.

MATTHEW [full of scorn for a man so ignorant as to be unable to pronounce the word Connaught, which practically rhymes with bonnet in Ireland, though in Hodson's dialect it rhymes with untaught]. Take care we don't cut the cable ourselves some day, bad scran to you! An tell me dhis: have yanny Coercion Acs in England? Have yanny removables? Have you Dublin Castle to suppress every newspaper dhat takes the part o your own counthry?

HODSON. We can beyave ahrselves withaht sich things.

MATTHEW. Bedad you're right. It'd only be waste o time to muzzle a sheep. Here! where's me pig? God forgimme for talkin to a poor ignorant craycher like you.

HODSON [grinning with good-humored malice, too convinced of his own superiority to feel his withers wrung]. Your pig'll ave a rare doin in that car, Paddy. Forty miles an ahr dahn that rocky lane will strike it pretty pink, you bet.

MATTHEW [scornfully]. Hwy can't you tell a raisonable lie when you're about it? What horse can go forty mile an hour?

HODSON. Orse! Wy, you silly oul rotten it's not a orse it's a mowtor. Do you suppose Tom Broadbent would gow off himself to arness a orse?

MATTHEW [in consternation]. Holy Moses! Don't tell me it's the ingine he wants to take me on.

HODSON. Wot else?

MATTHEW. Your sowl to Morris Kelly! why didn't you tell me that before? The divil an ingine he'll get me on this day. [His ear catches an approaching teuf-teuf] Oh murdher! it's comin afther me: I hear the puff puff of it. [He runs away through the gate, much to Hodson's amusement. The noise of the motor ceases; and Hodson, anticipating Broadbent's return, throws off the politician and recomposes himself as a valet. Broadbent and Larry come through the shrubbery. Hodson moves aside to the gate].

BROADBENT. Where is Mr Haffigan? Has he gone for the pig?

HODSON. Bolted, sir! Afraid of the motor, sir.

BROADBENT [much disappointed]. Oh, that's very tiresome. Did he leave any message?

HODSON. He was in too great a hurry, sir. Started to run home, sir, and left his pig behind him.

BROADBENT [eagerly]. Left the pig! Then it's all right. The pig's the thing: the pig will win over every Irish heart to me. We'll take the pig home to Haffigan's farm in the motor: it will have a tremendous effect. Hodson!

HODSON. Yes sir?

BROADBENT. Do you think you could collect a crowd to see the motor?

HODSON. Well, I'll try, sir.

BROADBENT. Thank you, Hodson: do.

Hodson goes out through the gate.

LARRY [desperately]. Once more, Tom, will you listen to me?

BROADBENT. Rubbish! I tell you it will be all right.

LARRY. Only this morning you confessed how surprised you were to find that the people here showed no sense of humor.

BROADBENT [suddenly very solemn]. Yes: their sense of humor is in abeyance: I noticed it the moment we landed. Think of that in a country where every man is a born humorist! Think of what it means! [Impressively] Larry we are in the presence of a great national grief.

LARRY. What's to grieve them?

BROADBENT. I divined it, Larry: I saw it in their faces. Ireland has never smiled since her hopes were buried in the grave of Gladstone.

LARRY. Oh, what's the use of talking to such a man? Now look here, Tom. Be serious for a moment if you can.

BROADBENT [stupent] Serious! I!!!

LARRY. Yes, you. You say the Irish sense of humor is in abeyance. Well, if you drive through Rosscullen in a motor car with Haffigan's pig, it won't stay in abeyance. Now I warn you.

BROADBENT [breezily]. Why, so much the better! I shall enjoy the joke myself more than any of them. [Shouting] Hallo, Patsy Farrell, where are you?

PATSY [appearing in the shrubbery]. Here I am, your honor.

BROADBENT. Go and catch the pig and put it into the car—we're going to take it to Mr Haffigan's. [He gives Larry a slap on the shoulders that sends him staggering off through the gate, and follows him buoyantly, exclaiming] Come on, you old croaker! I'll show you how to win an Irish seat.

PATSY [meditatively]. Bedad, if dhat pig gets a howlt o the handle o the machine— [He shakes his head ominously and drifts away to the pigsty].

ACT IV

THE parlor in Cornelius Doyle's house. It communicates with the garden by a half glazed door. The fireplace is at the other side of the room, opposite the door and windows, the architect not having been sensitive to draughts. The table, rescued from the garden, is in the middle; and at it sits Keegan, the central figure in a rather crowded apartment.

Nora, sitting with her back to the fire at the end of the table, is playing backgammon across its corner with him, on his left hand. Aunt Judy, a little further back, sits facing the fire knitting, with her feet on the fender. A little to Keegan's right, in front of the table, and almost sitting on it, is Barney Doran. Half a dozen friends of his, all men, are between him and the open door, supported by others outside. In the corner behind them is the sofa, of mahogany and horsehair, made up as a bed for Broadbent. Against the wall behind Keegan stands a mahogany sideboard. A door leading to the interior of the house is near the fireplace, behind Aunt Judy. There are chairs against the wall, one at each end of the sideboard. Keegan's hat is on the one nearest the inner door; and his stick is leaning against it. A third chair, also against the wall, is near the garden door.

There is a strong contrast of emotional atmosphere between the two sides of the room. Keegan is extraordinarily stern: no game of backgammon could possibly make a man's face so grim. Aunt Judy is quietly busy. Nora it trying to ignore Doran and attend to her game.

On the other hand Doran is reeling in an ecstasy of mischievous mirth which has infected all his friends. They are screaming with laughter, doubled up, leaning on the furniture and against the walls, shouting, screeching, crying.

AUNT JUDY [as the noise lulls for a moment]. Arra hold your noise, Barney. What is there to laugh at?

DORAN. It got its fut into the little hweel—[he is overcome afresh; and the rest collapse again].

AUNT JUDY. Ah, have some sense: you're like a parcel o childher. Nora, hit him a thump on the back: he'll have a fit.

DORAN [with squeezed eyes, exsuflicate with cachinnation] Frens, he sez to dhem outside Doolan's: I'm takin the gintleman that pays the rint for a dhrive.

AUNT JUDY. Who did he mean be that?

DORAN. They call a pig that in England. That's their notion of a joke.

AUNT JUDY. Musha God help them if they can joke no better than that!

DORAN [with renewed symptoms]. Thin—

AUNT JUDY. Ah now don't be tellin it all over and settin yourself off again, Barney.

NORA. You've told us three times, Mr Doran.

DORAN. Well but whin I think of it—!

AUNT JUDY. Then don't think of it, alanna.

DORAN. There was Patsy Farrll in the back sate wi dhe pig between his knees, n me bould English boyoh in front at the machinery, n Larry Doyle in the road startin the injine wid a bed winch. At the first puff of it the pig lep out of its skin and bled Patsy's nose wi dhe ring in its snout. [Roars of laughter: Keegan glares at them]. Before Broadbent knew hwere he was, the pig was up his back and over into his lap; and bedad the poor baste did credit to Corny's thrainin of it; for it put in the fourth speed wid its right crubeen as if it was enthered for the Gordn Bennett.

NORA [reproachfully]. And Larry in front of it and all! It's nothn to laugh at, Mr Doran.

DORAN. Bedad, Miss Reilly, Larry cleared six yards backwards at wan jump if he cleared an inch; and he'd a cleared seven if Doolan's granmother hadn't cotch him in her apern widhout intindin to. [Immense merriment].

AUNT JUDY, Ah, for shame, Barney! the poor old woman! An she was hurt before, too, when she slipped on the stairs.

DORAN. Bedad, ma'am, she's hurt behind now; for Larry bouled her over like a skittle. [General delight at this typical stroke of Irish Rabelaisianism].

NORA. It's well the lad wasn't killed.

DORAN. Faith it wasn't o Larry we were thinkin jus dhen, wi dhe pig takin the main sthreet o Rosscullen on market day at a mile a minnit. Dh ony thing Broadbint could get at wi dhe pig in front of him was a fut brake; n the pig's tail was undher dhat; so that whin he thought he was putn non the brake he was ony squeezin the life out o the pig's tail. The more he put the brake on the more the pig squealed n the fasther he dhruv.

AUNT JUDY. Why couldn't he throw the pig out into the road?

DORAN. Sure he couldn't stand up to it, because he was spanchelled-like between his seat and dhat thing like a wheel on top of a stick between his knees.

AUNT JUDY. Lord have mercy on us!

NORA. I don't know how you can laugh. Do you, Mr Keegan?

KEEGAN [grimly]. Why not? There is danger, destruction, torment! What more do we want to make us merry? Go on, Barney: the last drops of joy are not squeezed from the story yet. Tell us again how our brother was torn asunder.

DORAN [puzzled]. Whose bruddher?

KEEGAN. Mine.

NORA. He means the pig, Mr Doran. You know his way.

DORAN [rising gallantly to the occasion]. Bedad I'm sorry for your poor bruddher, Misther Keegan; but I recommend you to thry him wid a couple o fried eggs for your breakfast tomorrow. It was a case of Excelsior wi dhat ambitious baste; for not content wid jumpin from the back seat into the front wan, he jumped from the front wan into the road in front of the car. And—

KEEGAN. And everybody laughed!

NORA. Don't go over that again, please, Mr Doran.

DORAN. Faith be the time the car went over the poor pig dhere was little left for me or anywan else to go over except wid a knife an fork.

AUNT JUDY. Why didn't Mr Broadbent stop the car when the pig was gone?

DORAN. Stop the car! He might as well ha thried to stop a mad bull. First it went wan way an made fireworks o Molly Ryan's crockery stall; an dhen it slewed round an ripped ten fut o wall out o the corner o the pound. [With enormous enjoyment] Begob, it just tore the town in two and sent the whole dam market to blazes. [Nora offended, rises].

KEEGAN [indignantly]. Sir!

DORAN [quickly]. Savin your presence, Miss Reilly, and Misther Keegan's. Dhere! I won't say anuddher word.

NORA. I'm surprised at you, Mr Doran. [She sits down again].

DORAN [refectively]. He has the divil's own luck, that Englishman, annyway; for when they picked him up he hadn't a scratch on him, barrn hwat the pig did to his cloes. Patsy had two fingers out o jynt; but the smith pulled them sthraight for him. Oh, you never heard such a hullaballoo as there was. There was Molly, cryin Me chaney, me beautyful chaney! n oul Mat shoutin Me pig, me pig! n the polus takin the number o the car, n not a man in the town able to speak for laughin—

KEEGAN [with intense emphasis]. It is hell: it is hell. Nowhere else could such a scene be a burst of happiness for the people.

Cornelius comes in hastily from the garden, pushing his way through the little crowd.

CORNELIUS. Whisht your laughin, boys! Here he is. [He puts his hat on the sideboard, and goes to the fireplace, where he posts himself with his back to the chimneypiece].

AUNT JUDY. Remember your behavior, now.

Everybody becomes silent, solemn, concerned, sympathetic. Broadbent enters, roiled and disordered as to his motoring coat: immensely important and serious as to himself. He makes his way to the end of the table nearest the garden door, whilst Larry, who accompanies him, throws his motoring coat on the sofa bed, and sits down, watching the proceedings.

BROADBENT [taking off his leather cap with dignity and placing it on the table]. I hope you have not been anxious about me.

AUNT JUDY. Deedn we have, Mr Broadbent. It's a mercy you weren't killed.

DORAN. Kilt! It's a mercy dheres two bones of you left houldin together. How dijjescape at all at all? Well, I never thought I'd be so glad to see you safe and sound again. Not a man in the town would say less [murmurs of kindly assent]. Won't you come down to Doolan's and have a dhrop o brandy to take the shock off?

BROADBENT. You're all really too kind; but the shock has quite passed off.

DORAN [jovially]. Never mind. Come along all the same and tell us about it over a frenly glass.

BROADBENT. May I say how deeply I feel the kindness with which I have been overwhelmed since my accident? I can truthfully declare that I am glad it happened, because it has brought out the kindness and sympathy of the Irish character to an extent I had no conception of.

SEVERAL {Oh, sure you're welcome!

PRESENT. {Sure it's only natural.

{Sure you might have been kilt.

A young man, on the point of bursting, hurries out. Barney puts an iron constraint on his features.

BROADBENT. All I can say is that I wish I could drink the health of everyone of you.

DORAN. Dhen come an do it.

BROADBENT [very solemnly]. No: I am a teetotaller.

AUNT JUDY [incredulously]. Arra since when?

BROADBENT. Since this morning, Miss Doyle. I have had a lesson [he looks at Nora significantly] that I shall not forget. It may be that total abstinence has already saved my life; for I was astonished at the steadiness of my nerves when death stared me in the face today. So I will ask you to excuse me. [He collects himself for a speech]. Gentlemen: I hope the gravity of the peril through which we have all passed—for I know that the danger to the bystanders was as great as to the occupants of the car—will prove an earnest of closer and more serious relations between us in the future. We have had a somewhat agitating day: a valuable and innocent animal has lost its life: a public building has been wrecked: an aged and infirm lady has suffered an impact for which I feel personally responsible, though my old friend Mr Laurence Doyle unfortunately incurred the first effects of her very natural resentment. I greatly regret the damage to Mr Patrick Farrell's fingers; and I have of course taken care that he shall not suffer pecuniarily by his mishap. [Murmurs of admiration at his magnanimity, and A Voice "You're a gentleman, sir"]. I am glad to say that Patsy took it like an Irishman, and, far from expressing any vindictive feeling, declared his willingness to break all his fingers and toes for me on the same terms [subdued applause, and "More power to Patsy!"]. Gentlemen: I felt at home in Ireland from the first [rising excitement among his hearers]. In every Irish breast I have found that spirit of liberty [A cheery voice "Hear Hear"], that instinctive mistrust of the Government [A small pious voice, with intense expression, "God bless you, sir!"], that love of independence [A defiant voice, "That's it! Independence!"], that indignant sympathy with the cause of oppressed nationalities abroad [A threatening growl from all: the ground-swell of patriotic passion], and with the resolute assertion of personal rights at home, which is all but extinct in my own country. If it were legally possible I should become a naturalized Irishman; and if ever it be my good fortune to represent an Irish constituency in parliament, it shall be my first care to introduce a Bill legalizing such an operation. I believe a large section of the Liberal party would avail themselves of it. [Momentary scepticism]. I do. [Convulsive cheering]. Gentlemen: I have said enough. [Cries of "Go on"]. No: I have as yet no right to address you at all on political subjects; and we must not abuse the warmhearted Irish hospitality of Miss Doyle by turning her sittingroom into a public meeting.

DORAN [energetically]. Three cheers for Tom Broadbent, the future member for Rosscullen!

AUNT JUDY [waving a half knitted sock]. Hip hip hurray!

The cheers are given with great heartiness, as it is by this time, for the more humorous spirits present, a question of vociferation or internal rupture.

BROADBENT. Thank you from the bottom of my heart, friends.

NORA [whispering to Doran]. Take them away, Mr Doran [Doran nods].

DORAN. Well, good evenin, Mr Broadbent; an may you never regret the day you wint dhrivin wid Halligan's pig! [They shake hands]. Good evenin, Miss Doyle.

General handshaking, Broadbent shaking hands with everybody effusively. He accompanies them to the garden and can be heard outside saying Goodnight in every inflexion known to parliamentary candidates. Nora, Aunt Judy, Keegan, Larry, and Cornelius are left in the parlor. Larry goes to the threshold and watches the scene in the garden.

NORA. It's a shame to make game of him like that. He's a gradle more good in him than Barney Doran.

CORNELIUS. It's all up with his candidature. He'll be laughed out o the town.

LARRY [turning quickly from the doorway]. Oh no he won't: he's not an Irishman. He'll never know they're laughing at him; and while they're laughing he'll win the seat.

CORNELIUS. But he can't prevent the story getting about.

LARRY. He won't want to. He'll tell it himself as one of the most providential episodes in the history of England and Ireland.

AUNT JUDY. Sure he wouldn't make a fool of himself like that.

LARRY. Are you sure he's such a fool after all, Aunt Judy? Suppose you had a vote! which would you rather give it to? the man that told the story of Haffigan's pig Barney Doran's way or Broadbent's way?

AUNT JUDY. Faith I wouldn't give it to a man at all. It's a few women they want in parliament to stop their foolish blather.

BROADBENT [bustling into the room, and taking off his damaged motoring overcoat, which he put down on the sofa]. Well, that's over. I must apologize for making that speech, Miss Doyle; but they like it, you know. Everything helps in electioneering.

Larry takes the chair near the door; draws it near the table; and sits astride it, with his elbows folded on the back.

AUNT JUDY. I'd no notion you were such an orator, Mr Broadbent.

BROADBENT. Oh, it's only a knack. One picks it up on the platform. It stokes up their enthusiasm.

AUNT JUDY. Oh, I forgot. You've not met Mr Keegan. Let me introjooce you.

BROADBENT [shaking hands effusively]. Most happy to meet you, Mr Keegan. I have heard of you, though I have not had the pleasure of shaking your hand before. And now may I ask you—for I value no man's opinion more—what you think of my chances here.

KEEGAN [coldly]. Your chances, sir, are excellent. You will get into parliament.

BROADBENT [delighted]. I hope so. I think so. [Fluctuating] You really think so? You are sure you are not allowing your enthusiasm for our principles to get the better of your judgment?

KEEGAN. I have no enthusiasm for your principles, sir. You will get into parliament because you want to get into it badly enough to be prepared to take the necessary steps to induce the people to vote for you. That is how people usually get into that fantastic assembly.

BROADBENT [puzzled]. Of course. [Pause]. Quite so. [Pause]. Er— yes. [Buoyant again] I think they will vote for me. Eh? Yes?

AUNT JUDY. Arra why shouldn't they? Look at the people they DO vote for!

BROADBENT [encouraged]. That's true: that's very true. When I see the windbags, the carpet-baggers, the charlatans, the—the—the fools and ignoramuses who corrupt the multitude by their wealth, or seduce them by spouting balderdash to them, I cannot help thinking that an honest man with no humbug about him, who will talk straight common sense and take his stand on the solid ground of principle and public duty, must win his way with men of all classes.

KEEGAN [quietly]. Sir: there was a time, in my ignorant youth, when I should have called you a hypocrite.

BROADBENT [reddening]. A hypocrite!

NORA [hastily]. Oh I'm sure you don't think anything of the sort, Mr Keegan.

BROADBENT [emphatically]. Thank you, Miss Reilly: thank you.

CORNELIUS [gloomily]. We all have to stretch it a bit in politics: hwat's the use o pretendin we don't?

BROADBENT [stiffly]. I hope I have said or done nothing that calls for any such observation, Mr Doyle. If there is a vice I detest—or against which my whole public life has been a protest—it is the vice of hypocrisy. I would almost rather be inconsistent than insincere.

KEEGAN. Do not be offended, sir: I know that you are quite sincere. There is a saying in the Scripture which runs—so far as the memory of an oldish man can carry the words—Let not the right side of your brain know what the left side doeth. I learnt at Oxford that this is the secret of the Englishman's strange power of making the best of both worlds.

BROADBENT. Surely the text refers to our right and left hands. I am somewhat surprised to hear a member of your Church quote so essentially Protestant a document as the Bible; but at least you might quote it accurately.

LARRY. Tom: with the best intentions you're making an ass of yourself. You don't understand Mr Keegan's peculiar vein of humor.

BROADBENT [instantly recovering his confidence]. Ah! it was only your delightful Irish humor, Mr Keegan. Of course, of course. How stupid of me! I'm so sorry. [He pats Keegan consolingly on the back]. John Bull's wits are still slow, you see. Besides, calling me a hypocrite was too big a joke to swallow all at once, you know.

KEEGAN. You must also allow for the fact that I am mad.

NORA. Ah, don't talk like that, Mr Keegan.

BROADBENT [encouragingly]. Not at all, not at all. Only a whimsical Irishman, eh?

LARRY. Are you really mad, Mr Keegan?

AUNT JUDY [shocked]. Oh, Larry, how could you ask him such a thing?

LARRY. I don't think Mr Keegan minds. [To Keegan] What's the true version of the story of that black man you confessed on his deathbed?

KEEGAN. What story have you heard about that?

LARRY. I am informed that when the devil came for the black heathen, he took off your head and turned it three times round before putting it on again; and that your head's been turned ever since.

NORA [reproachfully]. Larry!

KEEGAN [blandly]. That is not quite what occurred. [He collects himself for a serious utterance: they attend involuntarily]. I heard that a black man was dying, and that the people were afraid to go near him. When I went to the place I found an elderly Hindoo, who told me one of those tales of unmerited misfortune, of cruel ill luck, of relentless persecution by destiny, which sometimes wither the commonplaces of consolation on the lips of a priest. But this man did not complain of his misfortunes. They were brought upon him, he said, by sins committed in a former existence. Then, without a word of comfort from me, he died with a clear-eyed resignation that my most earnest exhortations have rarely produced in a Christian, and left me sitting there by his bedside with the mystery of this world suddenly revealed to me.

BROADBENT. That is a remarkable tribute to the liberty of conscience enjoyed by the subjects of our Indian Empire.

LARRY. No doubt; but may we venture to ask what is the mystery of this world?

KEEGAN. This world, sir, is very clearly a place of torment and penance, a place where the fool flourishes and the good and wise are hated and persecuted, a place where men and women torture one another in the name of love; where children are scourged and enslaved in the name of parental duty and education; where the weak in body are poisoned and mutilated in the name of healing, and the weak in character are put to the horrible torture of imprisonment, not for hours but for years, in the name of justice. It is a place where the hardest toil is a welcome refuge from the horror and tedium of pleasure, and where charity and good works are done only for hire to ransom the souls of the spoiler and the sybarite. Now, sir, there is only one place of horror and torment known to my religion; and that place is hell. Therefore it is plain to me that this earth of ours must be hell, and that we are all here, as the Indian revealed to me—perhaps he was sent to reveal it to me to expiate crimes committed by us in a former existence.

AUNT JUDY [awestruck]. Heaven save us, what a thing to say!

CORNELIUS [sighing]. It's a queer world: that's certain.

BROADBENT. Your idea is a very clever one, Mr Keegan: really most brilliant: I should never have thought of it. But it seems to me—if I may say so—that you are overlooking the fact that, of the evils you describe, some are absolutely necessary for the preservation of society, and others are encouraged only when the Tories are in office.

LARRY. I expect you were a Tory in a former existence; and that is why you are here.

BROADBENT [with conviction]. Never, Larry, never. But leaving politics out of the question, I find the world quite good enough for me: rather a jolly place, in fact.

KEEGAN [looking at him with quiet wonder]. You are satisfied?

BROADBENT. As a reasonable man, yes. I see no evils in the world—except, of course, natural evils—that cannot be remedied by freedom, self-government, and English institutions. I think so, not because I am an Englishman, but as a matter of common sense.

KEEGAN. You feel at home in the world, then?

BROADBENT. Of course. Don't you?

KEEGAN [from the very depths of his nature]. No.

BROADBENT [breezily]. Try phosphorus pills. I always take them when my brain is overworked. I'll give you the address in Oxford Street.

KEEGAN [enigmatically: rising]. Miss Doyle: my wandering fit has come on me: will you excuse me?

AUNT JUDY. To be sure: you know you can come in n nout as you like.

KEEGAN. We can finish the game some other time, Miss Reilly. [He goes for his hat and stick.

NORA. No: I'm out with you [she disarranges the pieces and rises]. I was too wicked in a former existence to play backgammon with a good man like you.

AUNT JUDY [whispering to her]. Whisht, whisht, child! Don't set him back on that again.

KEEGAN [to Nora]. When I look at you, I think that perhaps Ireland is only purgatory, after all. [He passes on to the garden door].

NORA. Galong with you!

BROADBENT [whispering to Cornelius]. Has he a vote?

CORNELIUS [nodding]. Yes. An there's lots'll vote the way he tells them.

KEEGAN [at the garden door, with gentle gravity]. Good evening, Mr Broadbent. You have set me thinking. Thank you.

BROADBENT [delighted, hurrying across to him to shake hands]. No, really? You find that contact with English ideas is stimulating, eh?

KEEGAN. I am never tired of hearing you talk, Mr Broadbent.

BROADBENT [modestly remonstrating]. Oh come! come!

KEEGAN. Yes, I assure you. You are an extremely interesting man. [He goes out].

BROADBENT [enthusiastically]. What a nice chap! What an intelligent, interesting fellow! By the way, I'd better have a wash. [He takes up his coat and cap, and leaves the room through the inner door].

Nora returns to her chair and shuts up the backgammon board.

AUNT JUDY. Keegan's very queer to-day. He has his mad fit on him.

CORNELIUS [worried and bitter]. I wouldn't say but he's right after all. It's a contrairy world. [To Larry]. Why would you be such a fool as to let him take the seat in parliament from you?

LARRY [glancing at Nora]. He will take more than that from me before he's done here.

CORNELIUS. I wish he'd never set foot in my house, bad luck to his fat face! D'ye think he'd lend me 300 pounds on the farm, Larry? When I'm so hard up, it seems a waste o money not to mortgage it now it's me own.

LARRY. I can lend you 300 pounds on it.

CORNELIUS. No, no: I wasn't putn in for that. When I die and leave you the farm I should like to be able to feel that it was all me own, and not half yours to start with. Now I'll take me oath Barney Doarn's goin to ask Broadbent to lend him 500 pounds on the mill to put in a new hweel; for the old one'll harly hol together. An Haffigan can't sleep with covetn that corner o land at the foot of his medda that belongs to Doolan. He'll have to mortgage to buy it. I may as well be first as last. D'ye think Broadbent'd len me a little?

LARRY. I'm quite sure he will.

CORNELIUS. Is he as ready as that? Would he len me five hunderd, d'ye think?

LARRY. He'll lend you more than the land'll ever be worth to you; so for Heaven's sake be prudent.

CORNELIUS [judicially]. All right, all right, me son: I'll be careful. I'm goin into the office for a bit. [He withdraws through the inner door, obviously to prepare his application to Broadbent].

AUNT JUDY [indignantly]. As if he hadn't seen enough o borryin when he was an agent without beginnin borryin himself! [She rises]. I'll bory him, so I will. [She puts her knitting on the table and follows him out, with a resolute air that bodes trouble for Cornelius].

Larry and Nora are left together for the first time since his arrival. She looks at him with a smile that perishes as she sees him aimlessly rocking his chair, and reflecting, evidently not about her, with his lips pursed as if he were whistling. With a catch in her throat she takes up Aunt Judy's knitting, and makes a pretence of going on with it.

NORA. I suppose it didn't seem very long to you.

LARRY [starting]. Eh? What didn't?

NORA. The eighteen years you've been away.

LARRY. Oh, that! No: it seems hardly more than a week. I've been so busy—had so little time to think.

NORA. I've had nothin else to do but think.

LARRY. That was very bad for you. Why didn't you give it up? Why did you stay here?

NORA. Because nobody sent for me to go anywhere else, I suppose. That's why.

LARRY. Yes: one does stick frightfully in the same place, unless some external force comes and routs one out. [He yawns slightly; but as she looks up quickly at him, he pulls himself together and rises with an air of waking up and getting to work cheerfully to make himself agreeable]. And how have you been all this time?

NORA. Quite well, thank you.

LARRY. That's right. [Suddenly finding that he has nothing else to say, and being ill at ease in consequence, he strolls about the room humming a certain tune from Offenbach's Whittington].

NORA [struggling with her tears]. Is that all you have to say to me, Larry?

LARRY. Well, what is there to say? You see, we know each other so well.

NORA [a little consoled]. Yes: of course we do. [He does not reply]. I wonder you came back at all.

LARRY. I couldn't help it. [She looks up affectionately]. Tom made me. [She looks down again quickly to conceal the effect of this blow. He whistles another stave; then resumes]. I had a sort of dread of returning to Ireland. I felt somehow that my luck would turn if I came back. And now here I am, none the worse.

NORA. Praps it's a little dull for you.

LARRY. No: I haven't exhausted the interest of strolling about the old places and remembering and romancing about them.

NORA [hopefully]. Oh! You DO remember the places, then?

LARRY. Of course. They have associations.

NORA [not doubting that the associations are with her]. I suppose so.

LARRY. M'yes. I can remember particular spots where I had long fits of thinking about the countries I meant to get to when I escaped from Ireland. America and London, and sometimes Rome and the east.

NORA [deeply mortified]. Was that all you used to be thinking about?

LARRY. Well, there was precious little else to think about here, my dear Nora, except sometimes at sunset, when one got maudlin and called Ireland Erin, and imagined one was remembering the days of old, and so forth. [He whistles Let Erin Remember].

NORA. Did jever get a letter I wrote you last February?

LARRY. Oh yes; and I really intended to answer it. But I haven't had a moment; and I knew you wouldn't mind. You see, I am so afraid of boring you by writing about affairs you don't understand and people you don't know! And yet what else have I to write about? I begin a letter; and then I tear it up again. The fact is, fond as we are of one another, Nora, we have so little in common— I mean of course the things one can put in a letter— that correspondence is apt to become the hardest of hard work.

NORA. Yes: it's hard for me to know anything about you if you never tell me anything.

LARRY [pettishly]. Nora: a man can't sit down and write his life day by day when he's tired enough with having lived it.

NORA. I'm not blaming you.

LARRY [looking at her with some concern]. You seem rather out of spirits. [Going closer to her, anxiously and tenderly] You haven't got neuralgia, have you?

NORA. No.

LARRY [reassured]. I get a touch of it sometimes when I am below par. [absently, again strolling about] Yes, yes. [He begins to hum again, and soon breaks into articulate melody].

Though summer smiles on here for ever,
Though not a leaf falls from the tree,
Tell England I'll forget her never,
[Nora puts dawn the knitting and stares at him].
    O wind that blows across the sea.
[With much expression]
Tell England I'll forget her ne-e-e-e-ver
O wind that blows acro-oss—

[Here the melody soars out of his range. He continues falsetto, but changes the tune to Let Erin Remember]. I'm afraid I'm boring you, Nora, though you're too kind to say so.

NORA. Are you wanting to get back to England already?

LARRY. Not at all. Not at all.

NORA. That's a queer song to sing to me if you're not.

LARRY. The song! Oh, it doesn't mean anything: it's by a German Jew, like most English patriotic sentiment. Never mind me, my dear: go on with your work; and don't let me bore you.

NORA [bitterly]. Rosscullen isn't such a lively place that I am likely to be bored by you at our first talk together after eighteen years, though you don't seem to have much to say to me after all.

LARRY. Eighteen years is a devilish long time, Nora. Now if it had been eighteen minutes, or even eighteen months, we should be able to pick up the interrupted thread, and chatter like two magpies. But as it is, I have simply nothing to say; and you seem to have less.

NORA. I—[her tears choke her; but the keeps up appearances desperately].

LARRY [quite unconscious of his cruelty]. In a week or so we shall be quite old friends again. Meanwhile, as I feel that I am not making myself particularly entertaining, I'll take myself off. Tell Tom I've gone for a stroll over the hill.

NORA. You seem very fond of Tom, as you call him.

LARRY [the triviality going suddenly out of his voice]. Yes I'm fond of Tom.

NORA. Oh, well, don't let me keep you from him.

LARRY. I know quite well that my departure will be a relief. Rather a failure, this first meeting after eighteen years, eh? Well, never mind: these great sentimental events always are failures; and now the worst of it's over anyhow. [He goes out through the garden door].

Nora, left alone, struggles wildly to save herself from breaking down, and then drops her face on the table and gives way to a convulsion of crying. Her sobs shake her so that she can hear nothing; and she has no suspicion that she is no longer alone until her head and breast are raised by Broadbent, who, returning newly washed and combed through the inner door, has seen her condition, first with surprise and concern, and then with an emotional disturbance that quite upsets him.

BROADBENT. Miss Reilly. Miss Reilly. What's the matter? Don't cry: I can't stand it: you mustn't cry. [She makes a choked effort to speak, so painful that he continues with impulsive sympathy] No: don't try to speak: it's all right now. Have your cry out: never mind me: trust me. [Gathering her to him, and babbling consolatorily] Cry on my chest: the only really comfortable place for a woman to cry is a man's chest: a real man, a real friend. A good broad chest, eh? not less than forty-two inches—no: don't fuss: never mind the conventions: we're two friends, aren't we? Come now, come, come! It's all right and comfortable and happy now, isn't it?

NORA [through her tears]. Let me go. I want me hankerchief.

BROADBENT [holding her with one arm and producing a large silk handkerchief from his breast pocket]. Here's a handkerchief. Let me [he dabs her tears dry with it]. Never mind your own: it's too small: it's one of those wretched little cambric handkerchiefs—

NORA [sobbing]. Indeed it's a common cotton one.

BROADBENT. Of course it's a common cotton one—silly little cotton one—not good enough for the dear eyes of Nora Cryna—

NORA [spluttering into a hysterical laugh and clutching him convulsively with her fingers while she tries to stifle her laughter against his collar bone]. Oh don't make me laugh: please don't make me laugh.

BROADBENT [terrified]. I didn't mean to, on my soul. What is it? What is it?

NORA. Nora Creena, Nora Creena.

BROADBENT [patting her]. Yes, yes, of course, Nora Creena, Nora acushla [he makes cush rhyme to plush].

NORA. Acushla [she makes cush rhyme to bush].

BROADBENT. Oh, confound the language! Nora darling—my Nora—the Nora I love—

NORA [shocked into propriety]. You mustn't talk like that to me.

BROADBENT [suddenly becoming prodigiously solemn and letting her go]. No, of course not. I don't mean it—at least I do mean it; but I know it's premature. I had no right to take advantage of your being a little upset; but I lost my self-control for a moment.

NORA [wondering at him]. I think you're a very kindhearted man, Mr Broadbent; but you seem to me to have no self-control at all [she turns her face away with a keen pang of shame and adds] no more than myself.

BROADBENT [resolutely]. Oh yes, I have: you should see me when I am really roused: then I have TREMENDOUS self-control. Remember: we have been alone together only once before; and then, I regret to say, I was in a disgusting state.

NORA. Ah no, Mr Broadbent: you weren't disgusting.

BROADBENT [mercilessly]. Yes I was: nothing can excuse it: perfectly beastly. It must have made a most unfavorable impression on you.

NORA. Oh, sure it's all right. Say no more about that.

BROADBENT. I must, Miss Reilly: it is my duty. I shall not detain you long. May I ask you to sit down. [He indicates her chair with oppressive solemnity. She sits down wondering. He then, with the same portentous gravity, places a chair for himself near her; sits down; and proceeds to explain]. First, Miss Reilly, may I say that I have tasted nothing of an alcoholic nature today.

NORA. It doesn't seem to make as much difference in you as it would in an Irishman, somehow.

BROADBENT. Perhaps not. Perhaps not. I never quite lose myself.

NORA [consolingly]. Well, anyhow, you're all right now.

BROADBENT [fervently]. Thank you, Miss Reilly: I am. Now we shall get along. [Tenderly, lowering his voice] Nora: I was in earnest last night. [Nora moves as if to rise]. No: one moment. You must not think I am going to press you for an answer before you have known me for 24 hours. I am a reasonable man, I hope; and I am prepared to wait as long as you like, provided you will give me some small assurance that the answer will not be unfavorable.

NORA. How could I go back from it if I did? I sometimes think you're not quite right in your head, Mr Broadbent, you say such funny things.

BROADBENT. Yes: I know I have a strong sense of humor which sometimes makes people doubt whether I am quite serious. That is why I have always thought I should like to marry an Irishwoman. She would always understand my jokes. For instance, you would understand them, eh?

NORA [uneasily]. Mr Broadbent, I couldn't.

BROADBENT [soothingly]. Wait: let me break this to you gently, Miss Reilly: hear me out. I daresay you have noticed that in speaking to you I have been putting a very strong constraint on myself, so as to avoid wounding your delicacy by too abrupt an avowal of my feelings. Well, I feel now that the time has come to be open, to be frank, to be explicit. Miss Reilly: you have inspired in me a very strong attachment. Perhaps, with a woman's intuition, you have already guessed that.

NORA [rising distractedly]. Why do you talk to me in that unfeeling nonsensical way?

BROADBENT [rising also, much astonished]. Unfeeling! Nonsensical!

NORA. Don't you know that you have said things to me that no man ought to say unless—unless—[she suddenly breaks down again and hides her face on the table as before] Oh, go away from me: I won't get married at all: what is it but heartbreak and disappointment?

BROADBENT [developing the most formidable symptoms of rage and grief]. Do you mean to say that you are going to refuse me? that you don't care for me?

NORA [looking at him in consternation]. Oh, don't take it to heart, Mr

Br—

BROADBENT [flushed and almost choking]. I don't want to be petted and blarneyed. [With childish rage] I love you. I want you for my wife. [In despair] I can't help your refusing. I'm helpless: I can do nothing. You have no right to ruin my whole life. You—[a hysterical convulsion stops him].

NORA [almost awestruck]. You're not going to cry, are you? I never thought a man COULD cry. Don't.

BROADBENT. I'm not crying. I—I—I leave that sort of thing to your damned sentimental Irishmen. You think I have no feeling because I am a plain unemotional Englishman, with no powers of expression.

NORA. I don't think you know the sort of man you are at all. Whatever may be the matter with you, it's not want of feeling.

BROADBENT [hurt and petulant]. It's you who have no feeling. You're as heartless as Larry.

NORA. What do you expect me to do? Is it to throw meself at your head the minute the word is out o your mouth?

BROADBENT [striking his silly head with his fists]. Oh, what a fool! what a brute I am! It's only your Irish delicacy: of course, of course. You mean Yes. Eh? What? Yes, yes, yes?

NORA. I think you might understand that though I might choose to be an old maid, I could never marry anybody but you now.

BROADBENT [clasping her violently to his breast, with a crow of immense relief and triumph]. Ah, that's right, that's right: That's magnificent. I knew you would see what a first-rate thing this will be for both of us.

NORA [incommoded and not at all enraptured by his ardor]. You're dreadfully strong, an a gradle too free with your strength. An I never thought o whether it'd be a good thing for us or not. But when you found me here that time, I let you be kind to me, and cried in your arms, because I was too wretched to think of anything but the comfort of it. An how could I let any other man touch me after that?

BROADBENT [touched]. Now that's very nice of you, Nora, that's really most delicately womanly [he kisses her hand chivalrously].

NORA [looking earnestly and a little doubtfully at him]. Surely if you let one woman cry on you like that you'd never let another touch you.

BROADBENT [conscientiously]. One should not. One OUGHT not, my dear girl. But the honest truth is, if a chap is at all a pleasant sort of chap, his chest becomes a fortification that has to stand many assaults: at least it is so in England.

NORA [curtly, much disgusted]. Then you'd better marry an Englishwoman.

BROADBENT [making a wry face]. No, no: the Englishwoman is too prosaic for my taste, too material, too much of the animated beefsteak about her. The ideal is what I like. Now Larry's taste is just the opposite: he likes em solid and bouncing and rather keen about him. It's a very convenient difference; for we've never been in love with the same woman.

NORA. An d'ye mean to tell me to me face that you've ever been in love before?

BROADBENT. Lord! yes.

NORA. I'm not your first love?

BROADBENT. First love is only a little foolishness and a lot of curiosity: no really self-respecting woman would take advantage of it. No, my dear Nora: I've done with all that long ago. Love affairs always end in rows. We're not going to have any rows: we're going to have a solid four-square home: man and wife: comfort and common sense—and plenty of affection, eh [he puts his arm round her with confident proprietorship]?

NORA [coldly, trying to get away]. I don't want any other woman's leavings.

BROADBENT [holding her]. Nobody asked you to, ma'am. I never asked any woman to marry me before.

NORA [severely]. Then why didn't you if you're an honorable man?

BROADBENT. Well, to tell you the truth, they were mostly married already. But never mind! there was nothing wrong. Come! Don't take a mean advantage of me. After all, you must have had a fancy or two yourself, eh?

NORA [conscience-stricken]. Yes. I suppose I've no right to be particular.

BROADBENT [humbly]. I know I'm not good enough for you, Nora. But no man is, you know, when the woman is a really nice woman.

NORA. Oh, I'm no better than yourself. I may as well tell you about it.

BROADBENT. No, no: let's have no telling: much better not. I shan't tell you anything: don't you tell ME anything. Perfect confidence in one another and no tellings: that's the way to avoid rows.

NORA. Don't think it was anything I need be ashamed of.

BROADBENT. I don't.

NORA. It was only that I'd never known anybody else that I could care for; and I was foolish enough once to think that Larry—

HROADBENT [disposing of the idea at once]. Larry! Oh, that wouldn't have done at all, not at all. You don't know Larry as I do, my dear. He has absolutely no capacity for enjoyment: he couldn't make any woman happy. He's as clever as be-blowed; but life's too earthly for him: he doesn't really care for anything or anybody.

NORA. I've found that out.

BROADBENT. Of course you have. No, my dear: take my word for it, you're jolly well out of that. There! [swinging her round against his breast] that's much more comfortable for you.

NORA [with Irish peevishness]. Ah, you mustn't go on like that. I don't like it.

BROADBENT [unabashed]. You'll acquire the taste by degrees. You mustn't mind me: it's an absolute necessity of my nature that I should have somebody to hug occasionally. Besides, it's good for you: it'll plump out your muscles and make em elastic and set up your figure.

NORA. Well, I'm sure! if this is English manners! Aren't you ashamed to talk about such things?

BROADBENT [in the highest feather]. Not a bit. By George, Nora, it's a tremendous thing to be able to enjoy oneself. Let's go off for a walk out of this stuffy little room. I want the open air to expand in. Come along. Co-o-o-me along. [He puts her arm into his and sweeps her out into the garden as an equinoctial gale might sweep a dry leaf].

Later in the evening, the grasshopper is again enjoying the sunset by the great stone on the hill; but this time he enjoys neither the stimulus of Keegan's conversation nor the pleasure of terrifying Patsy Farrell. He is alone until Nora and Broadbent come up the hill arm in arm. Broadbent is still breezy and confident; but she has her head averted from him and is almost in tears].

BROADBENT [stopping to snuff up the hillside air]. Ah! I like this spot. I like this view. This would be a jolly good place for a hotel and a golf links. Friday to Tuesday, railway ticket and hotel all inclusive. I tell you, Nora, I'm going to develop this place. [Looking at her] Hallo! What's the matter? Tired?

NORA [unable to restrain her tears]. I'm ashamed out o me life.

BROADBENT [astonished]. Ashamed! What of?

NORA. Oh, how could you drag me all round the place like that, telling everybody that we're going to be married, and introjoocing me to the lowest of the low, and letting them shake hans with me, and encouraging them to make free with us? I little thought I should live to be shaken hans with be Doolan in broad daylight in the public street of Rosscullen.

BROADBENT. But, my dear, Doolan's a publican: a most influential man. By the way, I asked him if his wife would be at home tomorrow. He said she would; so you must take the motor car round and call on her.

NORA [aghast]. Is it me call on Doolan's wife!

BROADBENT. Yes, of course: call on all their wives. We must get a copy of the register and a supply of canvassing cards. No use calling on people who haven't votes. You'll be a great success as a canvasser, Nora: they call you the heiress; and they'll be flattered no end by your calling, especially as you've never cheapened yourself by speaking to them before—have you?

NORA [indignantly]. Not likely, indeed.

BROADBENT. Well, we mustn't be stiff and stand-off, you know. We must be thoroughly democratic, and patronize everybody without distinction of class. I tell you I'm a jolly lucky man, Nora Cryna. I get engaged to the most delightful woman in Ireland; and it turns out that I couldn't have done a smarter stroke of electioneering.

NORA. An would you let me demean meself like that, just to get yourself into parliament?

BROADBENT [buoyantly]. Aha! Wait till you find out what an exciting game electioneering is: you'll be mad to get me in. Besides, you'd like people to say that Tom Broadbent's wife had been the making of him—that she got him into parliament—into the Cabinet, perhaps, eh?

NORA. God knows I don't grudge you me money! But to lower meself to the level of common people

BROADBENT. To a member's wife, Nora, nobody is common provided he's on the register. Come, my dear! it's all right: do you think I'd let you do it if it wasn't? The best people do it. Everybody does it.

NORA [who has been biting her lip and looking over the hill, disconsolate and unconvinced]. Well, praps you know best what they do in England. They must have very little respect for themselves. I think I'll go in now. I see Larry and Mr Keegan coming up the hill; and I'm not fit to talk to them.

BROADBENT. Just wait and say something nice to Keegan. They tell me he controls nearly as many votes as Father Dempsey himself.

NORA. You little know Peter Keegan. He'd see through me as if I was a pane o glass.

BROADBENT. Oh, he won't like it any the less for that. What really flatters a man is that you think him worth flattering. Not that I would flatter any man: don't think that. I'll just go and meet him. [He goes down the hill with the eager forward look of a man about to greet a valued acquaintance. Nora dries her eyes, and turns to go as Larry strolls up the hill to her].

LARRY. Nora. [She turns and looks at him hardly, without a word. He continues anxiously, in his most conciliatory tone]. When I left you that time, I was just as wretched as you. I didn't rightly know what I wanted to say; and my tongue kept clacking to cover the loss I was at. Well, I've been thinking ever since; and now I know what I ought to have said. I've come back to say it.

NORA. You've come too late, then. You thought eighteen years was not long enough, and that you might keep me waiting a day longer. Well, you were mistaken. I'm engaged to your friend Mr Broadbent; and I'm done with you.

LARRY [naively]. But that was the very thing I was going to advise you to do.

NORA [involuntarily]. Oh you brute! to tell me that to me face.

LARRY [nervously relapsing into his most Irish manner]. Nora, dear, don't you understand that I'm an Irishman, and he's an Englishman. He wants you; and he grabs you. I want you; and I quarrel with you and have to go on wanting you.

NORA. So you may. You'd better go back to England to the animated beefsteaks you're so fond of.

LARRY [amazed]. Nora! [Guessing where she got the metaphor] He's been talking about me, I see. Well, never mind: we must be friends, you and I. I don't want his marriage to you to be his divorce from me.

NORA. You care more for him than you ever did for me.

LARRY [with curt sincerity]. Yes of course I do: why should I tell you lies about it? Nora Reilly was a person of very little consequence to me or anyone else outside this miserable little hole. But Mrs Tom Broadbent will be a person of very considerable consequence indeed. Play your new part well, and there will be no more neglect, no more loneliness, no more idle regrettings and vain-hopings in the evenings by the Round Tower, but real life and real work and real cares and real joys among real people: solid English life in London, the very centre of the world. You will find your work cut out for you keeping Tom's house and entertaining Tom's friends and getting Tom into parliament; but it will be worth the effort.

NORA. You talk as if I were under an obligation to him for marrying me.

LARRY. I talk as I think. You've made a very good match, let me tell you.

NORA. Indeed! Well, some people might say he's not done so badly himself.

LARRY. If you mean that you will be a treasure to him, he thinks so now; and you can keep him thinking so if you like.

NORA. I wasn't thinking o meself at all.

LARRY. Were you thinking of your money, Nora?

NORA. I didn't say so.

LARRY. Your money will not pay your cook's wages in London.

NORA [flaming up]. If that's true—and the more shame for you to throw it in my face if it IS true—at all events it'll make us independent; for if the worst comes to the worst, we can always come back here an live on it. An if I have to keep his house for him, at all events I can keep you out of it; for I've done with you; and I wish I'd never seen you. So goodbye to you, Mister Larry Doyle. [She turns her back on him and goes home].

LARRY [watching her as she goes]. Goodbye. Goodbye. Oh, that's so Irish! Irish both of us to the backbone: Irish, Irish, Irish—

Broadbent arrives, conversing energetically with Keegan.

BROADBENT. Nothing pays like a golfing hotel, if you hold the land instead of the shares, and if the furniture people stand in with you, and if you are a good man of business.

LARRY. Nora's gone home.

BROADBENT [with conviction]. You were right this morning, Larry. I must feed up Nora. She's weak; and it makes her fanciful. Oh, by the way, did I tell you that we're engaged?

LARRY. She told me herself.

BROADBENT [complacently]. She's rather full of it, as you may imagine. Poor Nora! Well, Mr Keegan, as I said, I begin to see my way here. I begin to see my way.

KEEGAN [with a courteous inclination]. The conquering Englishman, sir. Within 24 hours of your arrival you have carried off our only heiress, and practically secured the parliamentary seat. And you have promised me that when I come here in the evenings to meditate on my madness; to watch the shadow of the Round Tower lengthening in the sunset; to break my heart uselessly in the curtained gloaming over the dead heart and blinded soul of the island of the saints, you will comfort me with the bustle of a great hotel, and the sight of the little children carrying the golf clubs of your tourists as a preparation for the life to come.

BROADBENT [quite touched, mutely offering him a cigar to console him, at which he smiles and shakes his head]. Yes, Mr Keegan: you're quite right. There's poetry in everything, even [looking absently into the cigar case] in the most modern prosaic things, if you know how to extract it [he extracts a cigar for himself and offers one to Larry, who takes it]. If I was to be shot for it I couldn't extract it myself; but that's where you come in, you see [roguishly, waking up from his reverie and bustling Keegan goodhumoredly]. And then I shall wake you up a bit. That's where I come in: eh? d'ye see? Eh? eh? [He pats him very pleasantly on the shoulder, half admiringly, half pityingly]. Just so, just so. [Coming back to business] By the way, I believe I can do better than a light railway here. There seems to be no question now that the motor boat has come to stay. Well, look at your magnificent river there, going to waste.

KEEGAN [closing his eyes]. "Silent, O Moyle, be the roar of thy waters."

BROADBENT. You know, the roar of a motor boat is quite pretty.

KEEGAN. Provided it does not drown the Angelus.

BROADBENT [reassuringly]. Oh no: it won't do that: not the least danger. You know, a church bell can make a devil of a noise when it likes.

KEEGAN. You have an answer for everything, sir. But your plans leave one question still unanswered: how to get butter out of a dog's throat.

BROADBENT. Eh?

KEEGAN. You cannot build your golf links and hotels in the air. For that you must own our land. And how will you drag our acres from the ferret's grip of Matthew Haffigan? How will you persuade Cornelius Doyle to forego the pride of being a small landowner? How will Barney Doran's millrace agree with your motor boats? Will Doolan help you to get a license for your hotel?

BROADBENT. My dear sir: to all intents and purposes the syndicate I represent already owns half Rosscullen. Doolan's is a tied house; and the brewers are in the syndicate. As to Haffigan's farm and Doran's mill and Mr Doyle's place and half a dozen others, they will be mortgaged to me before a month is out.

KEEGAN. But pardon me, you will not lend them more on their land than the land is worth; so they will be able to pay you the interest.

BROADBENT. Ah, you are a poet, Mr Keegan, not a man of business.

LARRY. We will lend everyone of these men half as much again on their land as it is worth, or ever can be worth, to them.

BROADBENT. You forget, sir, that we, with our capital, our knowledge, our organization, and may I say our English business habits, can make or lose ten pounds out of land that Haffigan, with all his industry, could not make or lose ten shillings out of. Doran's mill is a superannuated folly: I shall want it for electric lighting.

LARRY. What is the use of giving land to such men? they are too small, too poor, too ignorant, too simpleminded to hold it against us: you might as well give a dukedom to a crossing sweeper.

BROADBENT. Yes, Mr Keegan: this place may have an industrial future, or it may have a residential future: I can't tell yet; but it's not going to be a future in the hands of your Dorans and Haffigans, poor devils!

KEEGAN. It may have no future at all. Have you thought of that?

BROADBENT. Oh, I'm not afraid of that. I have faith in Ireland, great faith, Mr Keegan.

KEEGAN. And we have none: only empty enthusiasms and patriotisms, and emptier memories and regrets. Ah yes: you have some excuse for believing that if there be any future, it will be yours; for our faith seems dead, and our hearts cold and cowed. An island of dreamers who wake up in your jails, of critics and cowards whom you buy and tame for your own service, of bold rogues who help you to plunder us that they may plunder you afterwards. Eh?

BROADBENT [a little impatient of this unbusinesslike view]. Yes, yes; but you know you might say that of any country. The fact is, there are only two qualities in the world: efficiency and inefficiency, and only two sorts of people: the efficient and the inefficient. It don't matter whether they're English or Irish. I shall collar this place, not because I'm an Englishman and Haffigan and Co are Irishmen, but because they're duffers and I know my way about.

KEEGAN. Have you considered what is to become of Haffigan?

LARRY. Oh, we'll employ him in some capacity or other, and probably pay him more than he makes for himself now.

BROADBENT [dubiously]. Do you think so? No no: Haffigan's too old. It really doesn't pay now to take on men over forty even for unskilled labor, which I suppose is all Haffigan would be good for. No: Haffigan had better go to America, or into the Union, poor old chap! He's worked out, you know: you can see it.

KEEGAN. Poor lost soul, so cunningly fenced in with invisible bars!

LARRY. Haffigan doesn't matter much. He'll die presently.

BROADBENT [shocked]. Oh come, Larry! Don't be unfeeling. It's hard on Haffigan. It's always hard on the inefficient.

LARRY. Pah! what does it matter where an old and broken man spends his last days, or whether he has a million at the bank or only the workhouse dole? It's the young men, the able men, that matter. The real tragedy of Haffigan is the tragedy of his wasted youth, his stunted mind, his drudging over his clods and pigs until he has become a clod and a pig himself—until the soul within him has smouldered into nothing but a dull temper that hurts himself and all around him. I say let him die, and let us have no more of his like. And let young Ireland take care that it doesn't share his fate, instead of making another empty grievance of it. Let your syndicate come—

BROADBENT. Your syndicate too, old chap. You have your bit of the stock.

LARRY. Yes, mine if you like. Well, our syndicate has no conscience: it has no more regard for your Haffigans and Doolans and Dorans than it has for a gang of Chinese coolies. It will use your patriotic blatherskite and balderdash to get parliamentary powers over you as cynically as it would bait a mousetrap with toasted cheese. It will plan, and organize, and find capital while you slave like bees for it and revenge yourselves by paying politicians and penny newspapers out of your small wages to write articles and report speeches against its wickedness and tyranny, and to crack up your own Irish heroism, just as Haffigan once paid a witch a penny to put a spell on Billy Byrne's cow. In the end it will grind the nonsense out of you, and grind strength and sense into you.

BROADBENT [out of patience]. Why can't you say a simple thing simply,

Larry, without all that Irish exaggeration and talky-talky? The syndicate is a perfectly respectable body of responsible men of good position. We'll take Ireland in hand, and by straightforward business habits teach it efficiency and self-help on sound Liberal principles. You agree with me, Mr Keegan, don't you?

KEEGAN. Sir: I may even vote for you.

BROADBENT [sincerely moved, shaking his hand warmly]. You shall never regret it, Mr Keegan: I give you my word for that. I shall bring money here: I shall raise wages: I shall found public institutions, a library, a Polytechnic [undenominational, of course], a gymnasium, a cricket club, perhaps an art school. I shall make a Garden city of Rosscullen: the round tower shall be thoroughly repaired and restored.

KEEGAN. And our place of torment shall be as clean and orderly as the cleanest and most orderly place I know in Ireland, which is our poetically named Mountjoy prison. Well, perhaps I had better vote for an efficient devil that knows his own mind and his own business than for a foolish patriot who has no mind and no business.

BROADBENT [stiffly]. Devil is rather a strong expression in that connexion, Mr Keegan.

KEEGAN. Not from a man who knows that this world is hell. But since the word offends you, let me soften it, and compare you simply to an ass. [Larry whitens with anger].

BROADBENT [reddening]. An ass!

KEEGAN [gently]. You may take it without offence from a madman who calls the ass his brother—and a very honest, useful and faithful brother too. The ass, sir, is the most efficient of beasts, matter-of-fact, hardy, friendly when you treat him as a fellow-creature, stubborn when you abuse him, ridiculous only in love, which sets him braying, and in politics, which move him to roll about in the public road and raise a dust about nothing. Can you deny these qualities and habits in yourself, sir?

BROADBENT [goodhumoredly]. Well, yes, I'm afraid I do, you know.

KEEGAN. Then perhaps you will confess to the ass's one fault.

BROADBENT. Perhaps so: what is it?

KEEGAN. That he wastes all his virtues—his efficiency, as you call it—in doing the will of his greedy masters instead of doing the will of Heaven that is in himself. He is efficient in the service of Mammon, mighty in mischief, skilful in ruin, heroic in destruction. But he comes to browse here without knowing that the soil his hoof touches is holy ground. Ireland, sir, for good or evil, is like no other place under heaven; and no man can touch its sod or breathe its air without becoming better or worse. It produces two kinds of men in strange perfection: saints and traitors. It is called the island of the saints; but indeed in these later years it might be more fitly called the island of the traitors; for our harvest of these is the fine flower of the world's crop of infamy. But the day may come when these islands shall live by the quality of their men rather than by the abundance of their minerals; and then we shall see.

LARRY. Mr Keegan: if you are going to be sentimental about Ireland, I shall bid you good evening. We have had enough of that, and more than enough of cleverly proving that everybody who is not an Irishman is an ass. It is neither good sense nor good manners. It will not stop the syndicate; and it will not interest young Ireland so much as my friend's gospel of efficiency.

BROADBENT. Ah, yes, yes: efficiency is the thing. I don't in the least mind your chaff, Mr Keegan; but Larry's right on the main point. The world belongs to the efficient.

KEEGAN [with polished irony]. I stand rebuked, gentlemen. But believe me, I do every justice to the efficiency of you and your syndicate. You are both, I am told, thoroughly efficient civil engineers; and I have no doubt the golf links will be a triumph of your art. Mr Broadbent will get into parliament most efficiently, which is more than St Patrick could do if he were alive now. You may even build the hotel efficiently if you can find enough efficient masons, carpenters, and plumbers, which I rather doubt. [Dropping his irony, and beginning to fall into the attitude of the priest rebuking sin] When the hotel becomes insolvent [Broadbent takes his cigar out of his mouth, a little taken aback], your English business habits will secure the thorough efficiency of the liquidation. You will reorganize the scheme efficiently; you will liquidate its second bankruptcy efficiently [Broadbent and Larry look quickly at one another; for this, unless the priest is an old financial hand, must be inspiration]; you will get rid of its original shareholders efficiently after efficiently ruining them; and you will finally profit very efficiently by getting that hotel for a few shillings in the pound. [More and more sternly] Besides those efficient operations, you will foreclose your mortgages most efficiently [his rebuking forefinger goes up in spite of himself]; you will drive Haffigan to America very efficiently; you will find a use for Barney Doran's foul mouth and bullying temper by employing him to slave-drive your laborers very efficiently; and [low and bitter] when at last this poor desolate countryside becomes a busy mint in which we shall all slave to make money for you, with our Polytechnic to teach us how to do it efficiently, and our library to fuddle the few imaginations your distilleries will spare, and our repaired Round Tower with admission sixpence, and refreshments and penny-in-the-slot mutoscopes to make it interesting, then no doubt your English and American shareholders will spend all the money we make for them very efficiently in shooting and hunting, in operations for cancer and appendicitis, in gluttony and gambling; and you will devote what they save to fresh land development schemes. For four wicked centuries the world has dreamed this foolish dream of efficiency; and the end is not yet. But the end will come.

BROADBENT [seriously]. Too true, Mr Keegan, only too true. And most eloquently put. It reminds me of poor Ruskin—a great man, you know. I sympathize. Believe me, I'm on your side. Don't sneer, Larry: I used to read a lot of Shelley years ago. Let us be faithful to the dreams of our youth [he wafts a wreath of cigar smoke at large across the hill].

KEEGAN. Come, Mr Doyle! is this English sentiment so much more efficient than our Irish sentiment, after all? Mr Broadbent spends his life inefficiently admiring the thoughts of great men, and efficiently serving the cupidity of base money hunters. We spend our lives efficiently sneering at him and doing nothing. Which of us has any right to reproach the other?

BROADBENT [coming down the hill again to Keegan's right hand]. But you know, something must be done.

KEEGAN. Yes: when we cease to do, we cease to live. Well, what shall we do?

BROADBENT. Why, what lies to our hand.

KEEGAN. Which is the making of golf links and hotels to bring idlers to a country which workers have left in millions because it is a hungry land, a naked land, an ignorant and oppressed land.

BROADBENT. But, hang it all, the idlers will bring money from England to Ireland!

KEEGAN. Just as our idlers have for so many generations taken money from Ireland to England. Has that saved England from poverty and degradation more horrible than we have ever dreamed of? When I went to England, sir, I hated England. Now I pity it. [Broadbent can hardly conceive an Irishman pitying England; but as Larry intervenes angrily, he gives it up and takes to the bill and his cigar again]

LARRY. Much good your pity will do it!

KEEGAN. In the accounts kept in heaven, Mr Doyle, a heart purified of hatred may be worth more even than a Land Development Syndicate of Anglicized Irishmen and Gladstonized Englishmen.

LARRY. Oh, in heaven, no doubt! I have never been there. Can you tell me where it is?

KEEGAN. Could you have told me this morning where hell is? Yet you know now that it is here. Do not despair of finding heaven: it may be no farther off.

LARRY [ironically]. On this holy ground, as you call it, eh?

KEEGAN [with fierce intensity]. Yes, perhaps, even on this holy ground which such Irishmen as you have turned into a Land of Derision.

BROADBENT [coming between them]. Take care! you will be quarrelling presently. Oh, you Irishmen, you Irishmen! Toujours Ballyhooly, eh? [Larry, with a shrug, half comic, half impatient, turn away up the hill, but presently strolls back on Keegan's right. Broadbent adds, confidentially to Keegan] Stick to the Englishman, Mr Keegan: he has a bad name here; but at least he can forgive you for being an Irishman.

KEEGAN. Sir: when you speak to me of English and Irish you forget that I am a Catholic. My country is not Ireland nor England, but the whole mighty realm of my Church. For me there are but two countries: heaven and hell; but two conditions of men: salvation and damnation. Standing here between you the Englishman, so clever in your foolishness, and this Irishman, so foolish in his cleverness, I cannot in my ignorance be sure which of you is the more deeply damned; but I should be unfaithful to my calling if I opened the gates of my heart less widely to one than to the other.

LARRY. In either case it would be an impertinence, Mr Keegan, as your approval is not of the slightest consequence to us. What use do you suppose all this drivel is to men with serious practical business in hand?

BROADBENT. I don't agree with that, Larry. I think these things cannot be said too often: they keep up the moral tone of the community. As you know, I claim the right to think for myself in religious matters: in fact, I am ready to avow myself a bit of a—of a—well, I don't care who knows it—a bit of a Unitarian; but if the Church of England contained a few men like Mr Keegan, I should certainly join it.

KEEGAN. You do me too much honor, sir. [With priestly humility to Larry] Mr Doyle: I am to blame for having unintentionally set your mind somewhat on edge against me. I beg your pardon.

LARRY [unimpressed and hostile]. I didn't stand on ceremony with you: you needn't stand on it with me. Fine manners and fine words are cheap in Ireland: you can keep both for my friend here, who is still imposed on by them. I know their value.

KEEGAN. You mean you don't know their value.

LARRY [angrily]. I mean what I say.

KEEGAN [turning quietly to the Englishman] You see, Mr Broadbent, I only make the hearts of my countrymen harder when I preach to them: the gates of hell still prevail against me. I shall wish you good evening. I am better alone, at the Round Tower, dreaming of heaven. [He goes up the hill].

LARRY. Aye, that's it! there you are! dreaming, dreaming, dreaming, dreaming!

KEEGAN [halting and turning to them for the last time]. Every dream is a prophecy: every jest is an earnest in the womb of Time.

BROADBENT [reflectively]. Once, when I was a small kid, I dreamt I was in heaven. [They both stare at him]. It was a sort of pale blue satin place, with all the pious old ladies in our congregation sitting as if they were at a service; and there was some awful person in the study at the other side of the hall. I didn't enjoy it, you know. What is it like in your dreams?

KEEGAN. In my dreams it is a country where the State is the Church and the Church the people: three in one and one in three. It is a commonwealth in which work is play and play is life: three in one and one in three. It is a temple in which the priest is the worshipper and the worshipper the worshipped: three in one and one in three. It is a godhead in which all life is human and all humanity divine: three in one and one in three. It is, in short, the dream of a madman. [He goes away across the hill].

BROADBENT [looking after him affectionately]. What a regular old Church and State Tory he is! He's a character: he'll be an attraction here. Really almost equal to Ruskin and Carlyle.

LARRY. Yes; and much good they did with all their talk!

BROADBENT. Oh tut, tut, Larry! They improved my mind: they raised my tone enormously. I feel sincerely obliged to Keegan: he has made me feel a better man: distinctly better. [With sincere elevation] I feel now as I never did before that I am right in devoting my life to the cause of Ireland. Come along and help me to choose the site for the hotel.

The Echo Library
www.echo-library.com

Please visit our website to download a complete catalogue of our books. We specialise in out-of-copyright reprints in all subjects. We publish a range of Large Print Editions of classic titles.

Books for re-printing

Suggestions for re-printing can be sent to titles@echo-library.com. Titles must be out-of-copyright or you must own the copyright. They can be in digital or published form.

If we do not wish to add the title to our catalogue then we can reprint for you. Costs depend on the format of the manuscript or book and its size.

Feedback

Because we have no direct contact with our customers we would welcome constructive comments to feedback@echo-library.com

Complaints

If there is a serious error in the text or layout please advise us by sending details to complaints@echo-library.com and we will supply a corrected copy, usually within 15 working days (it may take longer outside the UK and USA).

If there is a printing fault or the book is damaged please refer to your supplier.

Lightning Source UK Ltd.
Milton Keynes UK
UKHW011811201019
351963UK00001B/129/P